What readers are saying about
Practices of an Agile Developer

The "What It Feels Like" sections are just gold—it's one thing to tell someone to do this; it's quite another to put it into practice and know you're doing it right.

► **Nathaniel T. Schutta**
Coauthor, *Foundations of Ajax*

The book is what I've come to expect from the Pragmatic Bookshelf: short, easy to read, to the point, deep, insightful and useful. It should be a valuable resource for people wanting to do "agile."

► **Forrest Chang**
Software Lead

When I started reading *Practices of an Agile Developer*, I kept thinking, "Wow, a lot of developers need this book." It did not take long to realize that *I* needed this book. I highly recommend it to developers of all experience levels.

► **Guerry A. Semones**
Senior Software Engineer, Appistry

Practices of an Agile Developer uses common sense and experience to illustrate why you should consider adopting agile practices on your projects. This is precisely the kind of real-world, experiential information that is most difficult to glean from a book.

► **Matthew Johnson**
Principal Software Engineer

I was familiar with some of the practices mentioned since I own other books from the Pragmatic Bookshelf, but this book brings a lot of those ideas together and presents them in a clear, concise, organized format. I would highly recommend this book to a new developer or to a development team that wanted to get "agile."

► **Scott Splavec**
Senior Software Engineer

With agile practices spreading across the industry, there is a growing need to understand what it really means to be "agile." This book is a concise and practical guide to becoming just that.

► **Marty Haught**
Software Engineer/Architect, Razorstream

Maybe you have heard before about agile methodologies and have been asking yourself, what things can I do to improve my work each day? My answer would be to read this book and let the angels inside whisper in your ears the best personal practices you can embrace.

► **David Lázaro Saz**
Software Developer

This is a remarkably comprehensive yet targeted and concise overview of the core practices of agility. What I like best about this book is that it doesn't promote a specific agile methodology but rather ties together the practices common to each methodology into a coherent whole. This is required reading for anyone hungering for a faster, more reliable way to develop wickedly good software.

► **Matthew Bass**
Software Consultant

The perfect sequel to *The Pragmatic Programmer*!

► **Bil Kleb**
Research Scientist, NASA

Practices of an Agile Developer

Working in the Real World

Practices of an Agile Developer

Working in the Real World

Venkat Subramaniam

Andy Hunt

The Pragmatic Bookshelf

Raleigh, North Carolina   Dallas, Texas

Pragmatic
Bookshelf

Many of the designations used by manufacturers and sellers to distinguish their products are claimed as trademarks. Where those designations appear in this book, and The Pragmatic Programmers, LLC was aware of a trademark claim, the designations have been printed in initial capital letters or in all capitals. The Pragmatic Starter Kit, The Pragmatic Programmer, Pragmatic Programming, Pragmatic Bookshelf and the linking *g* device are trademarks of The Pragmatic Programmers, LLC.

Every precaution was taken in the preparation of this book. However, the publisher assumes no responsibility for errors or omissions, or for damages that may result from the use of information (including program listings) contained herein.

Our Pragmatic courses, workshops, and other products can help you and your team create better software and have more fun. For more information, as well as the latest Pragmatic titles, please visit us at

http://www.pragmaticprogrammer.com

ISBN 0-9745140-8-X

Printed on acid-free paper with 85% recycled, 30% post-consumer content.

Fourth printing, January 2008

Version: 2007-12-29

To our families and their inexhaustible patience.

கற்க கசடறக் கற்பவை கற்றபின்
நிற்க அதற்குத் தக.
திருக்குறள்-391

"Learn thoroughly what you learn;
let your conduct be worthy of what is learnt."
Verse 391 from *Thirukural, Collection of 1330 noble couplets*
Thiruvalluvar, poet and philosopher, 31 B.C.

Almost every wise saying
has an opposite one,
no less wise,
to balance it.

—George Santayana

Contents

*No matter how far down the wrong road
you've gone, turn back.*
    ► Turkish proverb

Chapter 1

Agile Software Development

That Turkish proverb above is both simple and obvious—you'd think it would be a guiding force for software development. But all too often, developers (including your humble authors) continue down the wrong road in the misguided hope that it will be OK somehow. Maybe it's close enough. Maybe this isn't *really* as wrong a road as it feels. We might even get away with it now and then, if creating software were a linear, deterministic process—like the proverbial road. But it's not.

Instead, software development is more like surfing—it's a dynamic, ever-changing environment. The sea itself is unpredictable, risky, and there may be sharks in those waters.

But what makes surfing so challenging is that *every wave is different*. Each wave takes its unique shape and behavior based on its locale—a wave in a sandy beach is a lot different from a wave that breaks over a reef, for instance.

In software development, the requirements and challenges that come up during your project development are your waves—never ceasing and ever-changing. Like the waves, software projects take different shapes and pose different challenges depending on your domain and application. And sharks come in many different guises.

Your software project depends on the skills, training, and competence of all the developers on the team. Like a successful surfer, a successful developer is the one with (technical) fitness, balance, and agility. Agility in both cases means being able to quickly *adapt* to the unfolding situation, whether it's a wave that breaks sooner than expected or a design that breaks sooner than expected.

The Agile Manifesto

We are uncovering better ways of developing software by doing it and helping others do it. Through this work we have come to value:

- *Individuals and interactions* over processes and tools
- *Working software* over comprehensive documentation
- *Customer collaboration* over contract negotiation
- *Responding to change* over following a plan

That is, while there is value in the items on the right, we value the items on the left more.

Copyright 2001, the Agile Manifesto authors

See `agilemanifesto.org` for more information.

The Spirit of Agility

So what is agility, exactly, and where did this whole agile software development movement come from?

In February 2001, seventeen interested persons (including Andy) got together in Snowbird, Utah, to discuss an emerging trend of what was loosely being called *lightweight processes*.

We had all seen projects fail because of ponderous, artifact-heavy, and results-light processes. It seemed like there should be a better way to look at methodology—a way to focus on the important stuff and de-emphasize the less important stuff that seemed to take up a lot of valuable time with little benefit.

These seventeen folks coined the term *agile* and published the Agile Manifesto to describe a refocused approach to software development: an approach that emphasizes people, collaboration, responsiveness, and working software (see the sidebar on this page for the introduction to the manifesto).

The agile approach combines responsive, collaborative people with a focus on demonstrable, concrete goals (software that actually works). That's the spirit of agility. The practical emphasis of development shifts from a plan-based approach, where key events happen in individual, separate episodes, to a more natural, continuous style.

It's assumed that everyone on the team (and working with the team) are professionals who want a positive outcome from the project. They may not necessarily be *experienced* professionals yet, but they possess a professional attitude—everyone wants to do the best job they can.

If you have problems with absenteeism, slackers, or outright saboteurs, this is probably not the approach for you. You'll need something more heavy-handed, slower, and less productive. Otherwise, you can begin developing in the agile style.

That means you don't leave testing to the end of the project. You don't leave integration to the end of the month or stop gathering requirements and feedback as you begin to code.

Instead, you continue to perform all these activities throughout the life cycle of the project. In fact, since software is never really "done" as long as people continue to use it, it's arguable that these aren't even *projects* any-

Continuous development, not episodic

more. Development is continuous. Feedback is continuous. You don't have to wait for months to find out that something is wrong: you find out quickly, while it's still relatively easy to fix. And you fix it, right then and there.

That's what it's all about.

This idea of continuous, ongoing development is pervasive in agile methods. It includes the development life cycle itself but also technology skills learning, requirements gathering, product deployment, user training, and everything else. It encompasses all activities, at all levels.

Why? Because developing software is such a complex activity, anything substantive that you leave until later won't happen, won't hap-

Inject energy

pen well, or will grow worse and fester until it becomes unmanageable. A certain kind of friction increases, and things get harder to fix and harder to change. As with any friction, the only way to fight it effectively is to continually inject a little energy into the system (see "Software Entropy" in *The Pragmatic Programmer* [HT00]).

Some people raise the concern that agile development is just *crisis management* in disguise. It's not. Crisis management occurs when problems are left to fester until they become so large that you have to drop everything else you're doing to respond to the crisis immediately. This causes secondary crises, so now you have a vicious cycle of never-ending crisis and panic. That's precisely what you want to avoid.

Instead, you want to tackle small problems while they are still small, explore the unknown before you invest too much in it, and be prepared to admit you got it all wrong as soon as you discover the truth. You need to retool your thinking, your coding practices, and your teamwork. It's not hard to do, but it might feel different at first.

The Practice of Agility

A useful definition of *agility* might be as follows:

> Agile development uses feedback to make constant adjustments in a highly collaborative environment.

Here's a quick summary of what that means in practice and what life on an agile team looks like.

It's a team effort. Agile teams tend to be small or broken up into several small (ten or so people) teams. You mostly work very closely together, in the same war room (or bull pen) if possible, sharing the code and the necessary development tasks. You work closely with the client or customer who is paying for this software and show them the latest version of the system as early and as often as possible.

You get constant feedback from the code you're writing and use automation to continuously build and test the project. You'll notice that the code needs to change as you go along: while the functionality remains the same, you'll still need to redesign parts of the code to keep up. That's called *refactoring*, and it's an ongoing part of development—code is never really "done."

Work progresses in *iterations*: small blocks of time (a week or so) where you identify a set of features and implement them. You demo the iteration to the customer to get feedback (and make sure you're headed in the right direction) and release full versions to the user community as often as practical.

With this all in mind, we're going to take a closer look at the practices of agility in the following areas:

Chapter 2: Beginning Agility. Software development is all in your head. In this chapter, we'll explain what we mean by that and how to begin with an agile mind-set and good personal practices as a firm foundation for the remainder of the book.

Chapter 3: Feeding Agility. An agile project doesn't just sit there. It requires ongoing background practices that aren't part of development itself but are vitally important to the health of the team. We'll see what needs to be done to help keep your team and yourself growing and moving forward.

Chapter 4: Delivering What Users Want. No matter how well written, software is useless if it doesn't meet the users' needs. We'll take a look at practices and techniques to keep the users involved, learn from their experience with the system, and keep the project aligned with their real needs.

Chapter 5: Agile Feedback. Using feedback to correct the software and the development process is what keeps an agile team on course where others might flounder and crash. The best feedback comes from the code itself; this chapter examines how to get that feedback as well as how to get a better handle on the team's progress and performance.

Chapter 6: Agile Coding. Keeping code flexible and adaptable to meet an uncertain future is critical to agile success. This chapter outlines some practical, proven techniques to keep code clean and malleable and prevent it from growing into a monster.

Chapter 7: Agile Debugging. Debugging errors can chew through a lot of time on a project—time you can't afford to lose. See how to make your debugging more effective and save time on the project.

Chapter 8: Agile Collaboration. Finally, an agile developer can be only so effective; beyond that, you need an agile team. We'll show you the most effective practice we've found to help jell a team together, as well as other practices that help the team function on a day-to-day basis and grow into the future.

An Agile Toolkit

Throughout the text, we'll refer to some of the basic tools that are in common use on agile projects. Here's a quick introduction, in case some of these might be new to you. More information on these topics is available from the books listed in the bibliography.

Wiki. A Wiki (short for WikiWikiWeb) is a website that allows users to edit the content and create links to new content using just a web browser. Wikis are a great way to encourage collaboration, because everyone on the team can dynamically add and rearrange content as needed. For more on Wikis, see *The Wiki Way* (LC01).

Version control. Everything needed to build the project—all source code, documents, icons, build scripts, etc.—needs to be placed in the care of a version control system. Surprisingly, many teams still prefer to plop files on a shared network drive, but that's a pretty amateurish approach. For a detailed guide to setting up and using version control, see *Pragmatic Version Control Using CVS* (TH03) or *Pragmatic Version Control Using Subversion* (Mas05).

Unit testing. Using code to exercise code is a major source of developer feedback; we'll talk much more about that later in the book, but be aware that readily available frameworks handle most of the housekeeping details for you. To get started with unit testing, there's *Pragmatic Unit Testing in Java* (HT03) and *Pragmatic Unit Testing in C#* (HT04), and you'll find helpful recipes in *JUnit Recipes* (Rai04).

Build automation. Local builds on your own machine, as well as centrally run builds for the whole team, are completely automated and reproducible. Since these builds run all the time, this is also known as *continuous integration*. As with unit testing, there are plenty of free, open-source and commercial products that will take care of the details for you. All the tips and tricks to build automation (including using lava lamps) are covered in *Pragmatic Project Automation* (Cla04).

Finally, you can find a good reference to tie these basic environmental practices together in *Ship It!* (RG05).

The Devil and Those Pesky Details

If you've flipped through the book, you may have noticed that the introduction section of the tips features a small woodcut of the devil himself, tempting you into bad and careless habits. They look like this:

"Go ahead, take that shortcut. It will save you time, really. No one will ever know, and you can be done with this task and move on quickly. That's what it's all about."

Some of his taunts may seem absurd, like something out of Scott Adams's *Dilbert* cartoons and his archetypical "pointy-haired boss." But remember Mr. Adams takes a lot of input from his loyal readers.

Some may seem more outlandish than others, but they are all legitimate lines of thought that your authors have heard, seen in practice, or secretly thought. These are the temptations we face, the costly shortcut we try anyway, in the vain hope of saving time on the project.

To counter those temptations, there's another section at the end of each practice where we'll give you your own guardian angel, dispensing key advice that we think you should follow:

Start with the hardest. *Always tackle the most difficult problems first, and leave the simple one towards the end.*

And since the real world is rarely that black-and-white, we've included sections that describe what a particular practice should feel like and tips on how to implement it successfully and keep it in balance. They look like this:

What It Feels Like

This section describes what a particular practice *should* feel like. If you aren't experiencing it this way, you may need to revise how you're following a particular practice.

Keeping Your Balance

- It's quite possible to overdo or underdo a practice, and in these sections we'll try to give you advice to keep a practice in balance, as well as general tips to help make it work for you.

After all, too much of a good thing, or a good thing misapplied, can become very dangerous (all too often we've seen a so-called agile project fail because the team didn't keep a particular practice in balance). We want to make sure you get real benefits from these practices.

By following these practices and applying them effectively in the real world—with balance—you'll begin to see a positive change on your projects and in your team.

You'll be following the practices of an agile developer, and what's more, you'll understand the principles that drive them.

Acknowledgments

Every book you read is a tremendous undertaking and involves many more people behind the scenes than just your lowly authors.

We'd like to thank all the following people for helping make this book happen.

Thanks to Jim Moore for creating the cover illustration and to Kim Wimpsett for her outstanding copyediting (and any remaining errors are surely the fault of our last-minute edits).

A special thanks to Johannes Brodwall, Chad Fowler, Stephen Jenkins, Bil Kleb, and Wes Reisz for their insight and helpful contributions.

And finally, thanks to all our reviewers who graciously gave their time and talent to help make this a better book: Marcus Ahnve, Eldon Alameda, Sergei Anikin, Matthew Bass, David Bock, A. Lester Buck III, Brandon Campbell, Forrest Chang, Mike Clark, John Cook, Ed Gibbs, Dave Goodlad, Ramamurthy Gopalakrishnan, Marty Haught, Jack Herrington, Ron Jeffries, Matthew Johnson, Jason Hiltz Laforge, Todd Little, Ted Neward, James Newkirk, Jared Richardson, Frédérick Ros, Bill Rushmore, David Lázaro Saz, Nate Schutta, Matt Secoske, Guerry Semones, Brian Sletten, Mike Stok, Stephen Viles, Leif Wickland, and Joe Winter.

Venkat says:
I would like to thank Dave Thomas for being such a wonderful mentor. Without his guidance, encouragement, and constructive criticism this book would have stayed a great idea.

I'm blessed to have Andy Hunt as my coauthor; I've learned a great deal from him. He is not only technically savvy (a fact that any pragmatic programmer out there already knows) but has incredible expressive power and exceptional attitude. I have admired the Pragmatic Programmers in every step of making of this book—they've truly figured and mastered the right set of tools, techniques, and, above all, attitude that goes into publishing.

I thank Marc Garbey for his encouragement. The world can use more people with his sense of humor and agility—he's a great friend. My special thanks to the geeks (err, friends) I had the pleasure to hang out with on the road—Ben Galbraith, Brian Sletten, Bruce Tate, Dave Thomas, David Geary, Dion Almaer, Eitan Suez, Erik Hatcher, Glenn Vanderburg, Howard Lewis Ship, Jason Hunter, Justin Gehtland, Mark Richards, Neal Ford, Ramnivas Laddad, Scott Davis, Stu Halloway, and Ted Neward—you guys are awesome! I thank Jay Zimmerman (a.k.a. agile driver), director of NFJS, for his encouragement and providing an opportunity to express my ideas on agility to his clients.

I thank my dad for teaching me the right set of values, and to you, Mom, for you're my true inspiration. None of this would have been possible but for the patience and encouragement of my wife, Kavitha, and my sons, Karthik and Krupakar; thank you and love you.

Andy says:
Well, I think just about everyone has been thanked already, but I'd like to thank Venkat especially for inviting me to contribute to this book. I wouldn't have accepted that offer from just anyone, but Venkat has been there and done that. He *knows* how this stuff works.

I'd like to thank all the good agile folks from the Snowbird get-together. None of us invented agility, but everyone's combined efforts have certainly made it a growing and powerful force in the modern world of software development.

And of course, I'd like to thank my family for their support and understanding. It has been a long ride from the original *The Pragmatic Programmer* book, but it has been a fun one.

And now, on with the show.

He who chooses the beginning of a road
chooses the place it leads to.
　▶ Harry Emerson Fosdick

Chapter 2

Beginning Agility

Traditional books on software development methodology might start with the Roles you'll need on a project, followed by the many Artifacts you need to produce (documents, checklists, Gantt charts, and so on). After that you'll see the Rules, usually expressed in a somewhat "Thou Shalt..." format.[1] Well, we're not going to do any of that here. Welcome to agility, where we do things a bit differently.

For instance, one popular software methodology suggests you need to fulfill some thirty-five distinct roles on a project, ranging from architect to designer to coder to librarian. Agile methods take a different tack. You perform just one role: software developer. That's you. You do what's needed on the team, working closely with the customer to build software. Instead of relying on Gantt charts and stone tablets, agility relies on people.

Software development doesn't happen in a chart, an IDE, or a design tool; it happens in your head. But it's not alone. There's a lot of other stuff happening in there as well: your emotions, office politics, egos, memories, and a whole lot of other baggage. Because it's all mixed in together, things as ephemeral as *attitude* and *mood* can make a big difference.

And that's why it's important to pay attention to attitude: yours and the team's. A professional attitude focuses on positive outcomes for the project and the team, on personal and team growth, and on success. It's easy to fall into pursuing less noble goals, and in this chapter,

---

[1]Or the ever popular, "The System shall...."

we'll look at ways to stay focused on the real goals. Despite common distractions, you want to *Work for Outcome* (see how beginning on the next page).

Software projects seem to attract a lot of time pressure—pressure that encourages you to take that ill-advised shortcut. But as any experienced developer will tell you, *Quick Fixes Become Quicksand* (see how to avoid the problem starting on page 16).

Each one of us has a certain amount of ego. Some of us (not naming names here) have what might be charitably termed a very "healthy" amount of ego; when asked to solve a problem, we take pride in arriving at the solution. But that pride can sometimes blind our objectivity. You've probably seen design discussions turn into arguments about individuals and personalities, rather than sticking to the issues and ideas related to the problem at hand. It's much more effective to *Criticize Ideas, Not People* (it's on page 19).

Feedback is fundamental to agility; you need to make changes as soon as you realize that things are headed in the wrong direction. But it's not always easy to point out problems, especially if there may be political consequences. Sometimes you need courage to *Damn the Torpedoes, Go Ahead* (we'll explain when, starting on page 24).

Agility works only when you adopt a professional attitude toward your project, your job, and your career. Without the right attitude, these practices won't help all that much. But with the right attitude, you can reap the full benefits of this approach. Here are the practices and advice we think will help.

Work for Outcome

"The first and most important step in addressing a problem is to determine who caused it. Find that moron! Once you've established fault, then you can make sure the problem doesn't happen again. Ever."

Sometimes that old devil sounds so plausible. Certainly you want to make finding the culprit your top priority, don't you? The bold answer is no. Fixing the problem is the top priority.

You may not believe this, but not everyone always has the outcome of the project as their top priority. Not even you. Consider your first, "default" reaction when a problem arises.

You might inadvertently fuel the problem by saying things that will complicate things further, by casting blame, or by making people feel defensive. Instead, take the high road, and ask, "What can I do to solve this or make it better?" In an agile team, the focus is on outcomes. You want to focus on fixing the problem, instead of affixing the blame.

The worst kind of job you can have (other than cleaning up after the elephants at the circus) is to work with a bunch of highly reactive peo-

Blame doesn't fix bugs

ple. They don't seem interested in solving problems; instead, they take pleasure in talking about each other behind their backs. They spend all their energy pointing fingers and discussing who they can blame. Productivity tends to be pretty low in such teams. If you find yourself on such a team, don't walk away from it—run. At a minimum, redirect the conversation away from the negative blame game toward something more neutral, like sports or the weather ("So, how about those Yankees?").

On an agile team, the situation is different. If you go to an agile team member with a complaint, you'll hear, "OK, what can I do to help you with this?" Instead of brooding over the problem, they'll direct their efforts toward solving it. Their motive is clear; it's the outcome that's important, not the credit, the blame, or the ongoing intellectual superiority contest.

You can start this yourself. When a developer comes to you with a complaint or a problem, ask about the specifics and how you can help. Just that simple act makes it clear that you intend to be part of the

> ### Compliance Isn't Outcome
>
> Many standardization and process efforts focus on measuring and rating *compliance to process* on the rationale that if the process works and it can be proved that you followed it exactly, then all is right with the world.
>
> But the real world doesn't work that way. You can be ISO-9001 certified and produce perfect, lead-lined life jackets. You followed the documented process perfectly; too bad all the users drowned.
>
> Measuring compliance to process doesn't measure outcome. Agile teams value *outcome* over process.

solution, not the problem; this takes the wind out of negativism. You're here to help. People will then start to realize that when they approach you, you'll genuinely try to help solve problems. They can come to you to get things fixed and go elsewhere if they're still interested in whining.

If you approach someone for help and get a less than professional response, you can try to salvage the conversation. Explain exactly what you want, and make it clear that your goal is the solution, not the blame/credit contest.

Blame doesn't fix bugs. *Instead of pointing fingers, point to possible solutions. It's the positive outcome that counts.*

What It Feels Like

It feels safe to admit that you don't have the answer. A big mistake feels like a learning opportunity, not a witch hunt. It feels like the team is working together, not blaming each other.

Keeping Your Balance

- "It's not my fault" is rarely true. "It's all your fault" is usually equally incorrect.

- If you aren't making *any* mistakes, you're probably not trying hard enough.

- It's not helpful to have QA argue with developers whether a problem is a defect or an enhancement. It's often quicker to fix it than argue about it.

- If one team member misunderstood a requirement, an API call, or the decisions reached in the last meeting, then it's very likely other team members may have misunderstood as well. Make sure the whole team is up to speed on the issue.

- If a team member is repeatedly harming the team by their actions, then they are not acting in a professional manner. They aren't helping move the team toward a solution. In that case, they need to be removed from this team.[2]

- If the majority of the team (and especially the lead developers) don't act in a professional manner and aren't interested in moving in that direction, then you should remove yourself from the team and seek success elsewhere (which is a far better idea than being dragged into a "Death March" project [You99]).

---

[2]They don't need to be fired, but they don't need to be on this team. But be aware that moving and removing people is dangerous to the team's overall balance as well.

▶ Quick Fixes Become Quicksand

"You don't need to really understand that piece of code; it seems to work OK as is. Oh, but it just needs one small tweak. Just add one to the result, and it works. Go ahead and put that in; it's probably fine."

We've all been there. There's a bug, and there's time pressure. The quick fix seems to work—just add one or ignore that last entry in the list, and it works OK for now. But what happens next distinguishes good programmers from crude hackers.

The crude hacker leaves the code as is and quickly moves on to the next problem.

The good programmer will go to the next step and try to understand *why* that +1 is necessary, and—more important—what else is affected.

Now this might sound like a contrived, even silly, example, except that it really happened—on a large scale. A former client of Andy's had this very problem. None of the developers or architects understood the underlying data model of their domain, and over the course of several years the code base became littered with thousands of +1 and -1 corrections. Trying to add features or fix bugs in that mess was a hair-pulling nightmare (and indeed, many of the developers had gone bald by then).

But like most catastrophes, it didn't get like that all at once. Instead, it happened one quick fix at a time. Each quick fix—which ignored the pervasive, underlying problem—added up to a swamp-like morass of quicksand that eventually sucked the life out of the project.

Beware of land mines

Shallow hacks are the problem—those quick changes that you make under pressure without a deep understanding of the true problem and any possible consequences. It's easy to fall prey to this temptation: the quick fix is a very seductive proposition. With a short enough lens, *it looks like it works.* But in any longer view, you may as well be walking across a field strewn with land mines. You might make it halfway across—or even more—and everything seems fine. But sooner or later....

As soon as that quick hack goes in, the clarity of the code goes down. Once a number of those pile up, clarity is out the window, and opacity

Andy Says...

Understand Process, Too

Although we're talking about understanding code, and especially understanding code well before you make changes to it, the same argument holds for your team's methodology or development process.

You have to understand the development methodology in use on your team. You have to understand how the methodology in place is supposed to work, why things are the way they are, and how they got that way.

Only with that understanding can you begin to make changes effectively.

takes over. You've probably worked places where they say, "Whatever you do, don't touch that module of code. The guy who wrote it is no longer here, and no one knows how it works." There's no clarity. The code is opaque, and no one can understand it.

You can't possibly be agile with that kind of baggage. But some agile techniques can help prevent this from happening. We'll look at these in more depth in later chapters, but here's a preview.

Isolation is dangerous; don't let your developers write code in complete isolation (see Practice 40, *Practice Collective Ownership*, on page 158). If team members take the time to read the code that their colleagues write, they can ensure that it's readable and understandable—and isn't laced with arbitrary "+1s and -1s". The more frequently you read the code, the better. These ongoing *code reviews* not only help make the code understandable but they are also one of the most effective ways of spotting bugs (see Practice 44, *Review Code*, on page 168).

Don't code in isolation

The other major technique that can help prevent opaque code is unit testing. Unit testing helps you naturally layer the code into manageable pieces, which results in better designed, clearer code. Further into the project, you can go back and read the unit tests—they're a

Use unit tests

kind of executable documentation (see Practice 19, *Put Angels on Your Shoulders*, on page 81). Unit tests allow you to look at smaller, more comprehensible modules of code and help you get a thorough understanding by running and working with the code.

Don't fall for the quick hack. *Invest the energy to keep code clean and out in the open.*

What It Feels Like

It feels like the code is well lit; there are no dark corners in the project. You may not know every detail of every piece of code or every step of every algorithm, but you have a good general working knowledge. No code is cordoned off with police tape or "Keep Out" signs.

Keeping Your Balance

- You need to understand how a piece of code works, but you don't necessarily have to become an expert at it. Know enough to work with it effectively, but don't make a career of it.

- If a team member proclaims that a piece of code is too hard for anyone else to understand, then it will be too hard for anyone (including the original author) to maintain. Simplify it.

- Never kludge in a fix without understanding. The +1/-1 syndrome starts innocently enough but rapidly escalates into an opaque mess. Fix the problem, not the symptom.

- Most nontrivial systems are too complex for any one person to understand entirely. You need to have a high-level understanding of most of the parts in order to understand what pieces of the system interact with each other, in addition to a deeper understanding of the particular parts on which you're working.

- If the system has already become an opaque mess, follow the advice given in Practice 4, *Damn the Torpedoes, Go Ahead*, on page 24.

Criticize Ideas, Not People

"You have a lot invested in your design. You've put your heart and soul into it. You know it's better than anyone else's. Don't even bother listening to their ideas; they'll just confuse the issue."

You've probably seen design discussions that get out of hand and become emotionally charged—decisions get made based on whose idea it was, not on the merits of the ideas themselves. We've been in meetings like that, and they aren't pleasant.

But it's only natural. When Lee presents a new design, it's easiest to say, "That's stupid" (with the clear implication that Lee is stupid as well). It takes a little more effort to elaborate, "That's stupid; you forgot to make it thread-safe." And it actually takes real effort and thought to say the far more appropriate, "Thanks, Lee. But I'm curious, what will happen when two users log on at the same time?"

See the difference? Let's look at common responses to an obvious error:

- Dismiss the person as incompetent.
- Dismiss the idea by pointing out the obvious flaw.
- Ask your teammate to address your concern.

The first choice is a nonstarter. Even if Lee is a complete bozo and couldn't program his way out of a paper bag, pointing that out isn't going to advance his education any and will likely dissuade Lee from offering any more ideas in the future. Choice two is at least more focused, but it doesn't help Lee that much and could well backfire on you. Lee may well respond to the accusation of unsafe threading with something clever: "Oh, it doesn't need to be multithreaded. Because this is executing in the context of the Frozbot module, it's already running in its own thread." Ouch. Forgot about that Frozbot thing. Now *you* feel stupid, and Lee is annoyed that you thought he was a bozo.

That leaves choice three. No accusation, no judgment, just a simple clarification. It lets Lee identify the problem himself, instead of having it thrown in his face.[3] It's the start of a *conversation*, not an argument.

---

[3]That's a great technique in general: ask a leading question that allows someone to figure out the problem for themselves.

Venkat Says...

Keep It Professional, Not Personal

Years ago, on my first day on the job as a system administrator, a senior admin and I were working on installing some software. I accidentally pushed a button bringing down the server. Within seconds, several frustrated users were knocking on the door.

My mentor earned my trust and respect when—instead of pointing fingers—he said, "Sorry, we're trying to find what went wrong. The system should be up in a few minutes." I learned an important and unforgettable lesson.

In the tight confines of a development team, that small amount of politeness and courtesy goes a long way to help keep the team focused on the pure merits of an idea, not on distractions of personal politics. We all are capable of generating excellent, innovative ideas, and we are all equally capable of proposing some real turkeys.

If there's a substantial risk that your idea will be ridiculed or that you'll lose face for suggesting it, you won't be inclined to offer another suggestion. Ever. And that's a real problem: a good software development effort, and a good design, requires a lot of creativity and insight. The whole project benefits when people with different ideas and concerns share and merge those ideas into something larger than any individual contributor could offer.

Negativity kills innovation

Negative comments and attitudes kill innovation. Now, we're not suggesting that you and your team should hold hands and sing "Kumbaya" during your design meetings. It would slow the meeting down, for one thing. But you need to keep your focus on solving problems rather than trying to prove whose idea is better. Having only one highly talented person on a team is merely ineffective, but it's much worse to have a few clashing heads who refuse to work together. Productivity and innovation quickly dies on those teams.

We all have some good ideas and some bad ideas, and everyone on the team needs to feel free to express them. Even if your idea is not fully taken up, it may help shape the solution. Don't be afraid of being criti-

> ## The Communal Camel
>
> Group design can be very effective, but some of the best innovations come from single minds—individuals with a strong vision. If you're the one with the vision, you need to be *extremely* respectful of others' potential contributions. You're the gatekeeper. You need to hold to the vision, but you need to be mindful and incorporate good new ideas even if they weren't yours originally.
>
> At the other end of the spectrum is the lackluster committee that has to reach consensus on each and every design decision. When building a horse, such a committee tends to create a camel instead.
>
> We're not suggesting you limit yourself to design by consensus, but you shouldn't be held hostage by a chief architect who is deaf to new ideas. What we are suggesting is that you remember Aristotle's observation:
>
> "It is the mark of an educated mind to be able to entertain a thought without accepting it."

cized. Remember, everyone who became an expert started somewhere. In the words of Les Brown, "You don't have to be great to get started, but you have to get started to be great."

Here are some particular techniques that can help:

Set a deadline. If you're having a design meeting, or are just having trouble getting to a solution, set a hard deadline such as lunchtime or the end of the day. That kind of time boxing helps keep the team moving and keeps you from getting too hung up on an endless ideological debate. And try to be (dare we say) pragmatic about it: there may not be a *best* answer, just a more suitable solution. A deadline helps you make the hard choices so you can move on.

Argue the opposite. Each member of the team should realize that there are always trade-offs involved. One way to be objective about an issue is to argue enthusiastically for it—and then passionately against it.[4] The goal is to pick a solution that has the most pros and the fewest cons, and this is a good way to collect as many pros and cons as you can. It also helps take some of the emotion out of the process.

Use a mediator. At the start of a meeting, pick a mediator who will act as the decision maker for that session. Each person should be given an opportunity to present ideas and opinions on various aspects of the problem. The mediator is there to make sure everyone gets a chance to be heard and to keep the meeting moving forward. The mediator can prevent prima donnas from dominating the meeting and can step in to remedy thoughtless remarks.

It's easiest to step back and monitor the meeting when you aren't actively participating in the discussion itself, so the mediator should concentrate on mediating, not contributing ideas (and ideally shouldn't have a vested interest in the project's timeline). And of course, while technical skills aren't strictly required for this task, people skills are.

Support the decision. Once a solution is picked (by whatever means), each team member should switch gears and give their complete cooperation in seeing it through to implementation. Everyone has to keep in mind that the goal is to get the project working to meet your customers' needs. It doesn't matter to the customer whose idea it was—they care only that the application works and that it meets their expectations. It's the outcome that counts.

Design (and life, for that matter) is full of compromises. A winning team is the one that realizes this fact. Working together with the team *unemotionally* takes effort, but exhibiting such maturity among your team members won't go unnoticed. This is an area where leading by example pays off—the practice is contagious.

Criticize ideas, not people. Take pride in arriving at a solution rather than proving whose idea is better.

---

[4]See "Debating with Knives" at http://blogs.pragprog.com/cgi-bin/pragdave.cgi/Random/FishBowl.rdoc.

What It Feels Like

It feels comfortable when the team discusses the genuine merits and possible drawbacks of several candidate solutions. You can reject solutions that have too many drawbacks without hurt feelings, and imperfect (but still better) solutions can be adopted without guilt.

Keeping Your Balance

- Always try to contribute a good idea, but don't be upset if your ideas don't make it into the product. Don't add extra cruft to an existing good idea just to add your own input.

- The real debate usually ends up on how realistic the negative points are. It's easy to slam an idea you're biased against by raising negatives that might not ever happen or that aren't realistic. If this starts happening, ask whether the problem has ever happened before and how often it came up.

  In other words, it's not enough to say, "We can't adopt that strategy because the database vendor may go out of business," or "The users would never accept that idea." You have to also assess just how likely that scenario really is. If you have to prototype or research to back up or refute a position, do so.

- Before setting out to find the best solution, it might be a good idea to make sure everyone agrees on what *best* means in this context. The best thing for developers may not be the best for users, and vice versa.

- There is no absolute *best*, only *better*. Despite the popularity of the term, there is no such thing as "best practices," only better practices in a particular situation.

- Being unemotional does not mean you blindly accept any and all ideas presented. Choose the right words and reasons to explain why you can't see the merits of an idea or solution, and ask clarifying questions.

▶ 4 Damn the Torpedoes, Go Ahead

"When you discover a problem in someone else's code, just keep it to yourself. After all, you wouldn't want to hurt their feelings or cause trouble. And if that someone else happens to be your boss, be extra careful, and just follow orders."

In the fable "Who Will Bell the Cat?" the mice decide to tie a bell around the neck of the cat so they'd receive advance warning when the cat was on the prowl. Every mouse agrees that this is an excellent plan. The old mouse asks, "So, who will volunteer to tie on the bell?" Not surprisingly, no mouse stepped forward, and the plan was dropped.

Sometimes the best plans fail in the absence of courage. Despite the dangers—the real and metaphorical torpedoes—you need to charge ahead and do what's right.

You've just been asked to fix some code written by someone else. The code is very hard to understand and work with. Should you continue to work with it, leaving it in a mess at the end? Or should you tell the boss that the code sucks and should be thrown away?

Maybe it's cathartic to stomp around telling everyone how bad the code is, but that's just complaining, not working on a solution. Instead, present the pros and cons of working with the code versus rewriting it. Show—don't just tell—that it's more cost effective to throw the code away and rewrite it. Present reasons that will help your boss (and colleagues) evaluate the situation, helping them come to the correct solution.

Now suppose you've been working on a particular component for a while. Suddenly you realize that you've been climbing the wrong tree; you really should redo your work. Naturally, you're worried about confessing the problem to the rest of your team and asking for more time or for help.

Rather than trying to cover up the issue, stand up and say, "I now realize that what I've done is not the right approach. Here are some of the ways I thought of to fix it—if you have more ideas, I'd like to hear about them—but it's going to take more time." You have removed all heat out of the issue and clearly indicated that you're interested in finding a solution. You have asked people to work with you on a solution—there's no place for rebuttal. Your team will be motivated to

Venkat Says...

Enforce Good Practices

I was working with an application that sends different types of files to a server process and was asked to implement code to save another type of file. That shouldn't be hard. When I started digging in, I was shocked to find that the code to handle each type of file was duplicated. So I followed suit: I copied and pasted a hundred lines of code, changed two lines in it, and got it working in minutes—but I felt low. I had violated good working practices.

I convinced the boss that the code would quickly become too expensive to maintain and should be refactored. Within a week, we saw the benefit of that effort when we had to make some changes to how files were handled—only now, the change was contained to one place instead of spread all over the system.

work with you in solving the problem. They may step in and give you a hand. What's more, you've shown your honesty and courage—you've earned their trust.

You know the right thing that needs to be done—or at least that the current way is wrong. Have courage to explain your view to the rest of the team, your boss, or the client. That's not always easy, of course. It may be that this will make the project late, offend the project manager, or annoy the sponsors. You need to press forward and take the correct approach regardless.

It was Civil War Admiral David Farragut who famously said, "Damn the torpedoes! Captain Drayton, go ahead! Jouett, full speed!" Yes, there were mines in the way (called *torpedoes* at the time), but they had to get through, so full speed ahead they went.[5]

It was the right thing to do.

---

[5]In fact, Farragut's full quote is often simplified to the battle cry, "Damn the torpedoes, full speed ahead!"

Do what's right. *Be honest, and have the courage to communicate the truth. It may be difficult at times; that's why it takes courage.*

What It Feels Like

Courage doesn't feel very comfortable, certainly not ahead of time. But it's often the only way to remove obstacles that will just grow worse over time, and you'll feel relief instead of increasing dread.

Keeping Your Balance

- If you think the sky is falling and the rest of the team disagrees with you, consider that you might be right and that you haven't explained your reasoning well enough.

- If you think the sky is falling and the rest of the team disagrees with you, consider that they might be right.

- If design or code strikes you as odd, take the time to understand the reasons why the code is the way it is. If you then find the solution to be valid but confusing, you may only have to refactor to make it more meaningful. Don't start rejecting and rewriting simply because you can't understand it right away. That's not courage; that's impatience.

- If your courageous stand is met with resistance by decision makers who lack the necessary background to understand the situation, you need to present it to them in terms they will understand. "Cleaner code" is not likely to motivate businesspeople. Saving money, getting a good return on investment, avoiding lawsuits, and increasing the customer base are much better arguments.

- If you're being pressured to compromise code quality, it might help to point out that you, as a developer, don't have the authority to degrade corporate assets (the overall code base).

*Even if you are on the right track, you will
get run over if you just sit there.*
▶ Will Rogers

Chapter 3

Feeding Agility

Agility requires ongoing, background maintenance. As the Will Rogers quote above illustrates, you need to keep moving. While that was probably true as seen from the saddle of a horse, it's especially true for us programmers.

The software profession is an ever-changing and evolving field; although a few concepts are timeless, others quickly become obsolete. Being in the software profession is a bit like being on a treadmill—you have to keep up with the pace, or you'll get thrown off.

Who's going to help you keep up with the pace? Well, in the corporate world, only one person will look out for your interests—you. It's up to you to keep up with change.

Most new technologies are based on existing technologies and ideas. They'll add some new things, but the change is incremental. If you keep up, then handling each new thing is just a matter of recognizing the incremental change. If you don't keep up, technology change will appear sudden and insurmountable. It's like returning to your hometown after ten years: you notice a lot of change and may not even recognize some places. However, the folks who live there, and see small changes every day, are completely comfortable with it. We'll look at ways to *Keep Up with Change* on page 29.

Investing in keeping yourself up-to-date is a great start, but you also need to make an effort to *Invest in Your Team*, and we'll look at ways to do that starting on page 32.

Although learning new technology and new approaches is important, you'll need to let go of old, outdated approaches as well. In other words, you'll need to *Know When to Unlearn* (see how, beginning on page 35).

While we're on the subject of change, it's important to realize that your understanding changes over the course of the project. Things you thought you understood well may not be as clear as you thought. You need to constantly pursue those odd bits you don't quite understand, and we'll see how and why you should *Question Until You Understand* starting on page 38.

Finally, a well-oiled agile project team does many things on a regular, repeating basis. Once things get rolling, you can *Feel the Rhythm*, and we'll show you the beat on page 41.

Keep Up with Change

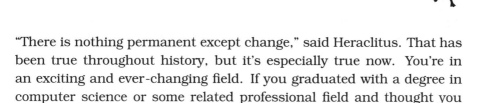

*"Technology changes so fast it's overwhelming. That's just the
nature of it. Stick to your old job with the language you know;
you can't possibly keep up."*

"There is nothing permanent except change," said Heraclitus. That has
been true throughout history, but it's especially true now. You're in
an exciting and ever-changing field. If you graduated with a degree in
computer science or some related professional field and thought you
were all done with learning, you were dead wrong.

Suppose you graduated in 1995, a mere ten years ago or so. What
did you know at the time? You probably knew C++ fairly well. You
saw some new language called Java. A concept called design patterns
was gaining interest. There was some talk about something called the
Internet. If you then went into hibernation and resurfaced in 2005,
what you'd see around you would be overwhelming. A year would not
be enough to learn all the new technologies and return to your former
level of proficiency, even within a fairly limited area of technology.

The pace at which technology evolves is incredible; take Java, for
instance. You have the Java language with its series of updated features. Then you have Swing, Servlets, JSP, Struts, Tapestry, JSF,
JDBC, JDO, Hibernate, JMS, EJB, Lucene, Spring...; the list goes on.
If you are into Microsoft technology, you have VB, Visual C++, MFC,
COM, ATL, .NET, C#, VB.NET, ASP.NET, ADO.NET, WinForms, Enterprise Services, Biztalk.... And don't forget UML, Ruby, XML, DOM, SAX,
JAXP, JDOM, XSL, Schema, SOAP, web services, SOA; yet again the list
goes on (and we're starting to run out of short acronyms).

Unfortunately, just having the right skills for the job at hand isn't sufficient anymore. That job won't even be available in another few years—it
will be outsourced or outdated, and you'll be out of a job.[1]

Suppose you were a Visual C++ or VB programmer, and you saw COM
come out. You spent time learning it (however painful that was), and
you kept up with what distributed object computing is all about. When
XML came out, you took time to learn that. You delved into ASP and

---

[1]See *My Job Went to India: 52 Ways to Save Your Job* [Fow05].

understood what it takes to develop a web application. You didn't become an expert on each of these technologies, but you didn't stay ignorant of them either. Your curiosity led you to find what MVC is and what design patterns are. You played around with Java a little bit to see what all the excitement was about.

If you had kept abreast of these technologies, then taking the next step and learning .NET is really not that big a deal. You didn't have to suddenly climb ten floors; you were climbing all along, and you likely had to step up just one or two floors at the end. If you stayed ignorant of all these technologies, then climbing up those ten floors would leave you out of breath at best. It would also take a long time—and all the while newer technologies would keep coming along.

How can you keep up with the pace? The good news is we have lots of technologies and facilities available today to help us continue our education. Here are some suggestions:

Learn iteratively and incrementally. Set aside some time every day for catching up. It doesn't have to be long, but it should be regular. Keep track of concepts you want to learn more about—just jot down a note when you hear some unfamiliar term or phrase. Then use your regularly scheduled time to investigate it further.

Get the latest buzz. The Web contains vast resources for learning about new technology. Read discussion forums and mailing lists to get a good flavor for the problems people are running into and the cool solutions they've discovered. Pick some well-established tech blogs and read them regularly—and check out what the top bloggers are reading (see http://pragmaticprogrammer.com for current suggestions).

Attend local user groups. Local user groups exist in many areas for Java, Ruby, Delphi, .NET, process improvement, OO design, Linux, Mac, and all manner of other technologies. Listen to the speakers, and plan on participating in the question-and-answer sessions afterward.

Attend workshops or conferences. Computer conferences are held all over the world, and many well-known consultants and authors conduct workshops and classes. These gatherings can be a great opportunity to learn directly from the experts.

Read voraciously. Find good books on software development and non-technical topics (we'd be happy to recommend a few), peer-reviewed journals and trade magazines, and even mass-media press (where it's fascinating to see old news presented as "cutting edge").

Keep up with changing technology. *You don't have to become an expert at everything, but stay aware of where the industry is headed, and plan your career and projects accordingly.*

What It Feels Like

You feel aware of what's going on; you know about technologies as they are announced and adopted. If you had to switch jobs into a new technology area, you could.

Keeping Your Balance

- Many new ideas never make it to full-fledged, useful technologies. The same is true for large, popular, well-funded endeavors. Gauge your effort.

- You can't be an expert at everything. Don't try. But once you're an expert at a few things, it becomes easier to gain expertise in selected new areas.

- Understand why a new technology is necessary—what problem is it trying to solve? Where can it be used?

- Avoid the impulse to convert your application to a newer technology, framework, or language just for sake of learning. You still have to evaluate the merits of a new technology before committing to it. Writing a small prototype might also be an effective antidote for overly extreme enthusiasm.

6 ▶ Invest in Your Team

"Don't share what you know—keep it to yourself. It's to your advantage to be the Smart One on the team. As long as you're smart, you can forget about those other losers."

Your team has developers with different capabilities, experience, and skills. Each person has different strengths and expertise. That mix of diverse talents and backgrounds makes it an ideal environment for learning.

On a team, it's not enough if you personally know a lot. If other members of your team are not as knowledgeable, the team isn't as effective as it could be: a well-educated team is a better team.

While working on projects, you need to use terms and metaphors to clearly communicate your design concepts and intent. If most members of your team are not familiar with these ideas, it will be hard for you to be effective. Also, suppose you've taken a course or gone to a symposium. You generally lose what you don't use. You need to bring what you have learned into your team. Share it with the rest of the team when you get back.

Find areas where you, or someone in your team who is knowledgeable, can help the rest of the team come up to speed (this has the added advantage that you can discuss how topics apply specifically to your applications or projects).

A "brown-bag session" is a great way to share knowledge in a team. Pick a day of the week, for instance Wednesday (generally any day other than Monday and Friday works well). Plan to get together over lunch so you don't have to worry about running into other meetings or getting special permission. Keep the cost low by having folks bring their own lunch (in a brown bag, of course).

Each week, ask one member of your team to lead the discussion. He or she will present some concepts, demo a tool, or do just about anything that's of interest to the team. You can pick a book and go through some specific sections, items, or practices from it.[2] Do whatever works.

---

[2]Pragmatic Bookshelf publishers Andy and Dave hear from a lot of folks who have set up reading groups to go through their books.

Is Everyone Better Than You? Good!

Legendary jazz guitarist Pat Metheny offers this advice: "Always be the worst guy in every band you're in. If you're the best guy there, you need to be in a different band. And I think that works for almost everything that's out there as well."

Why is that? If you're the best on the team, you have little incentive to continue to invest in yourself. But if everyone around you is better than you are, you'll be keenly motivated to catch up. You'll be on top of your game.

Plan to start with the person leading the session that week speaking for fifteen minutes or so. Then you can open the topic for discussion so everyone can present their ideas and discuss how the topic might be relevant to your projects. Discuss benefits, provide examples from your own applications, and plan to get follow-up information.

These brown-bag sessions can be very valuable. It raises the industry awareness of the whole team, and you can personally learn a lot from them as well. Wise managers tend to value team members who raise the value of other members, so presenting can directly help your career, as well.

 Raise the bar for you and your team. *Use brown-bag sessions to increase everyone's knowledge and skills and help bring people together. Get the team excited about technologies or techniques that will benefit your project.*

What It Feels Like

It feels like everyone is getting smarter. The whole team is aware of new technology and starts pointing out how to apply it or points out pitfalls to watch for.

Keeping Your Balance

- Reading groups that go through a book chapter by chapter are very helpful, but pick good books. *Learning XYZ in 7 Days with Patterns and UML* is probably not a good book.

- Not all the topics will be winners or even seem appropriate at the moment. Pay attention anyway; it wasn't raining when Noah built the ark.

- Try to keep it in the team. A catered lunch in the auditorium with PowerPoint slides loses some of the intimacy and discussion opportunities.

- Stick to a regular schedule. Constant, small exposure is agile. Infrequent, long, and drawn-out sessions are not.

- If some team members balk at coming to the lunch, bribe them with pizza.

- Stretch beyond purely technical books and topics; pertinent non-technical topics (project estimation, communication skills, etc.) will help the team as well.

- Brown-bag sessions aren't design meetings. Overall, you want to focus on discussing general topics that are relevant to your application. Solving specific issues is usually better left to a design meeting.

Know When to Unlearn

"That's the way you've always done it, and with good reason. It usually works for you just fine. The ways you learned when you first started are clearly the best ways. Not much has changed since then, really."

One of the foundations of agility is coping with change. Given that change is so constant and pervasive, does it make any sense to keep applying the same techniques and tools you've always used?

No, not really. We've spoken at length in this chapter about learning new technologies and approaches, but remember that you'll need to do some *un*learning as well.

As technology marches on, things that used to be of paramount importance fall by the wayside. Not only aren't they useful anymore, they can actually harm your effectiveness. When Andy was first programming, memory overlays were a big deal. You often couldn't fit the whole program in main memory (48KB or so) at a time, so you had to split your program into chunks. When one chunk was swapped in, some chunk had to be swapped out, and you couldn't call functions on one chunk from the other.

That very real constraint affects your design and coding techniques dramatically.

Back in the old days (when you could write about the artist known as Prince without resorting to a bitmap), you had to spend a lot of effort wringing extra cycles out of the processor by hand-tuning the assembly language output of the compiler. Can you picture yourself doing that in the context of some JavaScript or piece of J2EE code?

For most business applications, the technology has changed dramatically from the days of limited memory footprints, manual overlays, and hand-tuned assembly language.[3] But we've seen more than a few developers who never unlearned their old habits (and Prince, by the way, is once again known just as Prince).

Andy was once shown a piece of code that contained a single large **for** loop, written in C. The code inside the loop went on for sixty printed

---

[3]This can still be the case in some embedded systems development.

pages. The author "didn't trust" compiler optimizations and decided on doing loop unrolling and other tricks himself, by hand. Best of luck maintaining that mess.

Once upon a time, that might have been an acceptable trade-off. But not now. Machines and CPU cycles used to be the expensive part; now they are commodity. Developer time is now the scarce—and expensive—resource.

And that fact is slowly but surely dawning on people. We've seen ten-man-year J2EE projects go down in flames, only to be replaced with a month-long hack in PHP that delivers most of the features. Growing interest in languages such as PHP and web frameworks like Ruby on Rails (see [TH05]) show that developers are catching on that the old ways might not be cutting it anymore.

But unlearning can be hard. Many a team has floundered because management refused to spend $500 on a build machine, preferring instead to waste tens of thousands of dollars of programmers' time chasing down problems that shouldn't have even come up. That would have been the right answer when machines cost $500,000, but it's not the right answer now.

When learning a new technology, ask yourself whether you're projecting too much of the old attitudes and approaches onto the new. Learning to program in an object-oriented language is fundamentally different from programming in a procedural language. It's pretty easy to spot someone writing C code in Java, for instance, or VB in C# (or Fortran in anything). When that happens, you're losing the very advantage you hoped to gain by moving to the new technology.

Expensive mental models aren't discarded lightly.

Old habits are hard to break and even harder to notice. The first step to unlearning is to *realize* that you're using an outdated approach. That's the hardest part. The other hardest part is actually letting go. Mental models and patterns of thought are built and refined at great cost over many years. One doesn't discard them lightly.

And it's not that you really want to discard them completely, either. The previous memory overlay example is just a special case of manually maintaining a *working set* of items from a larger cache. The technique hasn't gone away, although that implementation of it has. You don't want to drill into the brain and snip all those dendrites off. Instead, you want to use older knowledge in context. Reinvent it and reuse it where applicable, but make sure you don't drag along old habits just out of, well, habit.

It can help if you take care to transition completely to the new environment as much as possible. For instance, when learning a new programming language, use the new IDE that comes with it instead of the plug-in that works with your old IDE. Write a completely different kind of application from the kind you usually write. Don't use your old language tools at all while you're transitioning. It's easier to form new associations and new habits when you have less baggage from the old habits lying around.

 Learn the new; unlearn the old. *When learning a new technology, unlearn any old habits that might hold you back. After all, there's much more to a car than just a horseless carriage.*

What It Feels Like

New technology feels a little scary. It feels like you have a lot to learn—and you do. You can use your existing skills and habits as a base, not as a crutch.

Keeping Your Balance

- The only difference between a rut and a grave is their dimensions. Keeping old habits past their expiration date is hazardous to your career.

- Don't forget the old habits completely, but use them only when using the appropriate related technology.

- Take special note of familiar idiosyncrasies in the languages you've worked with, and learn how these are similar or different in newer languages or versions.

8 ► Question Until You Understand

"Accept the explanation you've been given. If you're told where the problem lies, that's where you look. Don't waste your time chasing ghosts."

The last few tips have talked about improving your skills and those of your team. Here's one technique that almost always helps and will help with design, debugging, and requirements understanding as well.

Suppose there's a major problem in an application, and they call you in to fix it. You aren't familiar with the application, so they try to help you out, telling you the issue *must* be in one particular module—you can safely ignore the rest of the application. You have to figure out the problem quickly, while working with people whose patience may be wearing thin.

When the pressure is on like that, you might feel intimidated and not want to question too deeply what you've been told. To solve the problem, however, you need a good understanding of the big picture. You need to look at everything you think may be relevant—irrespective of what others may think.

Consider how a doctor works. When you're not well, the doctor asks you various questions—your habits, what you ate, where it hurts, what medication you've been taking, and so on. The human body is complex, and a lot of things can affect it. And unless the doctor is persistent, they may miss the symptoms completely.

For instance, a patient in New York City with a high fever, a rash, a severe headache, pain behind the eyes, and muscle and joint pain might be dismissed as having the flu, or possibly the measles. But by probing for the big picture, the doctor discovers the hapless patient just returned from a vacation to South America. Now instead of just the flu, a whole new world of possible diagnoses opens up—including dengue hemorrhagic fever.

Similarly, in a computer, a lot of issues can affect your application. You need to be aware of a number of factors in order to solve a problem. It's your responsibility to ask others to bear with you—have patience—as you ask any questions you think are relevant.

Or, suppose you're working with senior developers. They may have a better understanding of the system than you. But, they're human. They might miss things from time to time. Your questions may even help the rest of your team clarify their thinking; your fresh perspective and questions may give others a new perspective and lead them to find solutions for problems they have been struggling with.

"Why?" is a great question. In fact, in the popular management book *The Fifth Discipline: The Art and Practice of the Learning Organization* [Sen90], the author suggests asking no fewer than five progressive "Why?"s when trying to understand an issue. While that might sound like a policy oriented more toward an inquisitive four-year-old, it is a powerful way to dig past the simple, trite answers, the "party line," and the usual assumptions to get down to the truth of the matter.

The example given in the *Fifth Discipline Field Book* for this sort of root-cause analysis involves a consultant interviewing the manager at a manufacturing facility. On seeing an oil spill on the floor, the manager's first reaction is to order it cleaned up. But the consultant asks, "Why is there oil on the floor?" The manager, not quite getting the program, blames the cleaning crew for being inattentive. Again, the consultant asks, "Why is there oil on the floor?" Through a progressive series of "Whys" and a number of employees across different departments, the consultant finally isolated the real problem: a poorly worded purchasing policy that resulted in a massive purchase of defective gaskets.

The answer came as quite a shock to the manager and all the other parties involved; they had no idea. It brought a serious problem to light that would have festered and caused increasing damage otherwise. And all the consultant had to do was ask, "Why?"

"Oh, just reboot the system once a week, and you'll be fine." Really? Why? "You have to run the build three times in row to get a complete build." Really? Why? "Our users would never want that feature." Really? Why?

Why?

 Keep asking Why. *Don't just accept what you're told at face value. Keep questioning until you understand the root of the issue.*

What It Feels Like

It feels like mining for precious jewels. You sift through unrelated material, deeper and deeper, until you find the shining gem. You come to feel that you understand the real problem, not just the symptoms.

Keeping Your Balance

- You can get carried away and ask genuinely irrelevant questions— if your car won't start, asking about the tires probably isn't going to help. Ask "Why?" but keep it relevant.

- When you ask "Why?" you may well be asked, "Why do you ask?" in return. Keep a justification for your question in mind before you ask the question: this helps you keep your questions relevant.

- Don't settle for shallow answers. "Because it used to..." is probably not a good answer.

- "Gee, I don't know" is a good starting point for more research—not the end of the line.

Feel the Rhythm

"We haven't had a code review in a long time, so we're going to review everything all this week. Also, it's probably about time we made a release as well, so we picked three weeks from Tuesday for a next release."

On many less-than-successful projects, events happen on an irregular, haphazard basis. And that sort of random threat can be hard to deal with; you're never quite sure what's going to happen tomorrow or when the next all-hands-on-deck fire drill is going to occur.

But agile projects have rhythms and cycles that make life easier. For instance, Scrum protects the team from requirement changes during a thirty-day sprint. It's helpful to defer large-scale changes and handle them all at once.

Conversely, a lot of practices have to happen "all the time," that is, throughout the life of the project. It has been said that time is nature's way of keeping everything from happening all at once. Well, we need to take that one step further and keep a couple different rhythms going so that everything on an agile project doesn't happen all at once or happen at random, unpredictable times.

To begin with, consider the day itself. You'd like to end each day with some resolution, without having anything major hanging over your head. That's not always possible, of course, but you can plan on having all the code you're working on checked in and tested by the time you leave. If it's getting late in the day and the code you're working on just isn't amenable to getting done, perhaps it might be best to erase it and start over.

Now that sounds like pretty drastic advice, and maybe it is.[4] But as you're developing in small chunks, it can be helpful to time box yourself in this manner: if you don't have a good, working solution by a hard deadline (e.g., the end of the day), then maybe you should try a new tack. And it establishes a rhythm; at the end of most days, everything is checked in and tucked away. You can start the next day fresh and ready to tackle the next set of difficulties.

---

[4]Ron Jeffries tells us, "I wish people had the balls to do that more often."

Time Boxing

Agile developers get feedback from many sources: users, team members, and the code as it's tested. You use that feedback to help steer the project. But a very important form of feedback comes from time itself.

Many agile techniques rely on *time boxing*—setting a near-term, hard deadline for an activity that cannot be extended. You get to choose which other aspect will suffer, but the deadline is fixed. You probably don't know the exact number of time-boxes that are required to complete the overall task, but each individual box is short, is finite, and accomplishes a clear goal.

For example, iterations typically run a couple of weeks long. When the time is up, the iteration is done. That part is fixed—but the set of features that makes it into that particular iteration is flexible. In other words, you never slip the date, but you may slip a feature. Similarly, you may decide to time box a design meeting. That means at the end of the designated time, the meeting ends, and the design choices have been made.

A hard deadline forces you to make the hard choices. You can't waste time on philosophical discussions or features that are perpetually 80% done. A time box keeps you moving.

Sharks have to keep swimming, or they die. Software projects are like sharks in that respect; you need to keep moving with the best information you have available at the time.

The stand-up meeting (Practice 38, *Schedule Regular Face Time*, on page 151) is best held at the same time and in the same place every day, say around 10 a.m. or so. You start to get into the habit, and you have everything ready for the meeting at that time.

The biggest rhythm of all is the iteration length (Practice 17, *Use Short Iterations, Release in Increments*, on page 71), which should be something like one to four weeks long. Whatever length you choose, you should stick with it—a consistent length is important. That regular rhythm makes it easier to reach decisions and keep the project moving forward (see the sidebar on this page).

Tackle tasks before they bunch up. *It's easier to tackle common recurring tasks when you maintain steady, repeatable intervals between events.*

What It Feels Like

It feels like consistent, steady rhythm. Edit, run tests and review, over a consistent iteration length, and then release. It's easier to dance when you know when the next beat falls.

Keeping Your Balance

- Plan on having all code checked in and tested by the end of the day, with no leftovers.

- Don't let that trick you into working overtime constantly.

- Run the team's iterations (Practice 17, *Use Short Iterations, Release in Increments*, on page 71) at a fixed, regular length. You may need to adjust the length to find a comfortable value that works, but then you need to stick with it.

- A regular rhythm that's too intense will burn you out. Generally, as you interact with entities outside your team (or outside the organization), you need to adopt a slower rhythm. So-called Internet Time is probably too fast to be healthy.

- Regular rhythms make it harder to hide things; and help give you an excuse to have courage (see Practice 4, *Damn the Torpedoes, Go Ahead*, on page 24).

- As with losing weight, a little success is a great motivator. Small, reachable goals keep everyone moving forward. Make successes memorable by celebrating them: pizza and beer or a team lunch can help.

No plan survives contact with the enemy.
▶ Helmuth von Moltke

Chapter 4

Delivering What Users Want

Your customer gives you the requirements and expects you to deliver an application in a few years. You go off and build the system based on those requirements and eventually deliver it on time. The customer looks at it and says it is good. You move on to the next project with a very happy and loyal customer on your résumé. That's how your projects usually go, right?

That's not the case for most folks. It's more common to see users act shocked and/or unhappy. They don't like what they see, and they want many changes. They demand features that weren't in the requirements they originally gave you. Does that sound more like a typical project?

"No plan survives contact with the enemy," said von Moltke. The *enemy* in this case isn't the customer, the users, your teammates or management. The necessary enemy is change. In warfare, as in software development, the situation can change quickly and drastically. Sticking to yesterday's plan despite a change in circumstances is a recipe for disaster. You can't "defeat" change—whether it's the design, architecture, or your understanding of the user requirements. Agility—and successful development—hinges on your ability to identify and adapt to changes. Only then will we be able to develop on time and within budget, creating a system that actually meets the users' needs.

In this chapter we'll examine practices that lead toward these agile goals. To begin, we'll see why it's important to keep users and customers involved and *Let Customers Make Decisions* (starting on page 47). Design is a fundamental part of software development. You can't develop well without it, but you can't let it become a straitjacket either. See how to *Let Design Guide, Not Dictate*, beginning on page 50. And speaking of straitjackets, you'll want to make sure the technology you introduce on a project is appropriate. You'll need to *Justify Technology Use* (see how on page 54).

In order to keep your software accessible to users, it needs to be ready—always. To minimize disruptive changes from integrating new source, you'll *Integrate Early, Integrate Often* (that's on page 60). And it almost goes without saying that you don't want to break existing code; you want to always *Keep It Releasable* (that starts on page 57).

You can't waste any precious development time getting new features ready for users to look at over and over again, so you'll *Automate Deployment Early* (see how on page 63). By having code always ready to go and easy to deploy to users, you can *Get Frequent Feedback Using Demos* (it's on page 66). That allows you to release to the world at large on a more regular basis. You want to *Use Short Iterations, Release in Increments* to help stay fresh and close to the evolving user base (we'll start talking about that on page 71).

Finally, it can sometimes be difficult to get customers on board with the agile approach, especially if they demand a fixed-price contract up front. But the reality is that *Fixed Prices Are Broken Promises*, and we'll see how to work around that starting on page 75.

10 ▶ Let Customers Make Decisions

"Developers are creative and intelligent and know the most about the application. Therefore, developers should be making all the critical decisions. Anytime the businesspeople butt in, they just make a mess of things; they don't understand logic the way we do."

Developers must be involved in making design decisions. However, they shouldn't make *all* the decisions on a project, especially the business decisions.

Take the case of project manager Pat. Pat's project at a remote site was on track and within budget—it appeared to be a textbook example of a stellar project. Pat cheerfully took the code to the client site to demonstrate but came back crestfallen.

As it turned out, Pat's business analyst had fielded all the questions personally, rather than discussing them with the users. Business owners were not involved in the low-level decisions made throughout development. The project had a long way to go before completion, and *already* it fell short of the users' needs. The project had to be delayed and became yet another typical textbook example of project execution failure.

So you have a choice: either you can let the customers make the decisions now or they'll go ahead and make the decisions later—at much greater cost. If you avoid these issues during development, you increase risk; but by addressing these issues early, you avoid the possibility of significant design and code rework. You can also avoid mounting schedule pressure as you approach the project deadline.

For example, suppose you are working on a task. You think up two ways to implement it. One way is quicker but will limit what the users can do. The other way will take more time to implement but gives more flexibility to the users. You are obviously pressed for time (have you ever seen a project that isn't?), so should you just go with the first, quicker option? How do you decide? Toss a coin? Ask a colleague or your manager?

In one of Venkat's recent projects that faced a similar problem, the development manager decided in favor of the first option to save time. As you might guess, the customer was shocked—and furious—when these limitations surfaced during beta testing. The resulting rework cost the team much more money, time, and effort than necessary.

Decide what you shouldn't decide

The most important design decision a developer (and a manager) can make is to decide what's not in their hands and to let business owners make decisions on those issues. You don't want to have to make decisions that are business critical by yourself. After all, it's not your business. If the issue at hand affects the behavior of the system, or how it'll be used, take it to the business owner. If project leads, or managers, try to make those decisions by proxy, politely convince them it's better to take this up with the real business owners/customers (see Practice 4, *Damn the Torpedoes, Go Ahead*, on page 24).

When you talk to the customers, be prepared with the available options. Present them with the pros and cons and show the potential costs and the benefits—from the business point of view, not the technical point of view. Discuss the trade-offs and the impact of the options on the schedule and budget with them. Whatever decision they make, they'll have to live with it, so it's better that they can make it on an informed basis. If they want something else later, it's fair to renegotiate the cost and time for that change later.

Either way, it's their decision.

Let your customers decide. *Developers, managers, or business analysts shouldn't make business-critical decisions. Present details to business owners in a language they can understand, and let them make the decision.*

What It Feels Like

Business applications are developed as a partnership between the business owner and the developers. It should feel like a partnership—a good, honest working relationship.

Keeping Your Balance

- Keep records of decisions and the reasoning behind them. Memory is notoriously unreliable. An engineer's journal or log, a Wiki, an email trail, or an issue-tracking database are all acceptable, but take care that whatever method you choose doesn't become too heavy-weight or burdensome.

- Don't bug busy businesspeople with trivial low-level details. If it doesn't impact their business, it's trivial.

- Don't assume a low-level detail doesn't impact the business. If it can impact their business, it's not trivial.

- "I don't know" is a perfectly acceptable answer from a business owner. They may not have thought that far ahead yet or may need to see it in action to evaluate the issue. Advise them the best you can, and prepare the code for the eventual change.

Let Design Guide, Not Dictate

"Design documents should be as detailed as possible so that any lowly coder can just type in the code. Specify the high-level details of how objects are related, as well as lower-level details such as the interaction between objects. Be sure to include information on the implementations of methods and notes on their parameters. Don't forget all the fields of the class. Never deviate from the design, no matter what you discover while writing code."

"Design" is an essential step in the development process. It helps you understand details of the system, understand interrelationships between parts and subsystems, and directs you toward an implementation. Well-established methodologies emphasize design; some of them, such as the Unified Process, are quite ceremonial about producing related documents. Project managers and business owners often become obsessed with the details and want to make sure the system is fully designed and documented before coding starts. After all, that's how you'd manage a bridge or building construction project, isn't it?

On the other hand, agile methodologies recommend you start coding very early in the development phase. Does that imply there's no design?[1] Nope, not at all—it is still important to come up with a good design. It is essential to develop key diagrams (in UML, for example) that illustrate how the system will be organized in terms of classes and interactions. You need to take the time to think about (and discuss) the trade-offs, benefits, and pitfalls of the various options that come up during design.

Only then can you arrive at the structure you think should be coded. If you don't invest in that sort of thinking up front, you may become overwhelmed by nasty surprises once you start coding. Even in the construction analogy, it's common practice to rough-cut a piece of wood slightly longer than necessary and carefully trim it down to the final, perfect fit.

But even with a design in hand up front, some surprises will occur anyway. Keep in mind that the design you come up with at this stage is

---

[1]Refer to Martin Fowler's article "Is Design Dead?" (http://www.martinfowler.com/articles/designDead.html) for an excellent discussion of this topic.

> ### Being Exact
>
> "There's no sense being exact about something if you don't even know what you're talking about."—John von Neumann

based only on your *current* understanding of the requirements. All bets are off once you start coding. Designs, and the code that implements them, will constantly evolve.

Some project leads and managers think the design should be detailed enough to simply hand it off to "coders." They say the coder should not have to make any decisions but simply translate the design to code. Personally, neither of your authors would want to be the mere typist in this type of team. We suspect you wouldn't either.

What happens if designers craft their ideas in drawings and throw them across the chasm for programmers to code (see Practice 39, *Architects Must Write Code*, on page 155)? The programmers will be pressured to code these

Design should be only as detailed as needed to implement

designs/drawings exactly as they appear. What if the reality of the system and existing code indicates that this received design is not ideal? Too bad! Time has already been spent on design—there's no time left to go back and work on it again. The team soldiers on, implementing code they know to be wrong. Does that sound stupid? It should, and yet that's exactly how some companies choose to operate.

The idea of following a strict requirements-design-code-test sequence of tasks comes from a *waterfall*[2] mentality, which leads to overly detailed up-front design. Keeping the detailed, documented design up-to-date over the life of the project becomes a major undertaking and a huge investment in time and resources with very little payback. We can do better than that.

---

[2]*Waterfall approach* has come to mean following the sequential steps of defining the requirements in detail up front, followed by detailed design, then the implementation, then the integration, and finally testing (with your fingers crossed). That is not what the original author recommended; see [Roy70] for details.

There are two levels of design: *strategic* and *tactical*. The up-front design is strategic: you typically do that when you don't yet have a deep understanding of the requirements. That is, it should express a general strategy but not delve into precise details.

Strategic versus tactical design

This up-front, strategic level of design shouldn't specify the details of methods, parameters, fields, or the exact sequence of interaction between objects. That's left to the tactical design, and it unfolds only as the project evolves.

A good strategic design should act as a map that will point you in the right direction. Any design is only a starting point; you'll continue to develop and refine it further as you code over the project's lifetime.

Consider the epic journey of Lewis and Clark[3] across the United States in 1804. Their "design" was to cross the country. But they had no idea what they would face at any given point in the territory. They knew the goal and the constraints but not the details of the journey.

That's an apt analogy for design on a software project. Until you cross the territory itself, you can't reliably know what it's going to be like. So don't waste time setting the details of how you'll ford the river until you actually get to the riverbank and can evaluate it better. Only then can you realistically work on a tactical approach.

Instead of starting with a tactical design that focuses on individual methods or data types, it's more appropriate to discuss possible class designs in terms of responsibilities, because that is still a high-level, goal-oriented approach. In fact, the CRC card design method does just that. Classes are described in terms of the following:

- Class name

- Responsibilities—what is it supposed to do

- Collaborators—what other objects it works with to get the job done

How can you tell whether a design is good or even adequate? The best feedback on the nature of design comes from the code. If small changes in requirements remain easy to implement, then it's a good design. If small changes cause a large disruption or cause a disruption across a large swath of the code base, then the design needs improvement.

---

3. In the small-world department, Andy is related to William Clark.

A good design is a map; let it evolve. *Design points you in the right direction. It's not the territory itself; it shouldn't dictate the specific route. Don't let the design (or the designer) hold you hostage.*

What It Feels Like

A good design is accurate, but not precise. That is, what it says should be correct, but it shouldn't go far as to include details that might change or that are uncertain. It's an intent, not a recipe.

Keeping Your Balance

- "No Big Design Up Front" doesn't mean *no* design. It just means don't get stuck in a design task without validating it with real code. Diving into coding with no idea of a design is just as dangerous. Diving into code is fine for learning or prototyping, as long as you throw the code away afterward.

- Even though an initial design may end up being useless, you still have to do it: the act of creating the design is invaluable. As U.S. President Eisenhower said, "The *plan* is worthless. The *planning* is essential."[4] It's the learning that occurs during the design that's valuable, not necessarily the design itself.

- White boards, sketches and Post-it notes are excellent design tools. Complicated modeling tools have a tendency to be more distracting than illuminating.

---

[4]From a 1957 speech

Justify Technology Use

"You are starting a new project, with a laundry list of new technology and application frameworks in front of you. This is all great new stuff, and you really do need to use all of it. Think how great it will look on your résumé and how high-tech your new application will be with that great new framework."

Blindly picking a framework is like having kids to save taxes

Once upon a time, co-worker Lisa explained her proposed application to Venkat: she was planning on using Enterprise Java Beans (EJB). Venkat expressed some concern as to how EJB would be applicable to that particular project, and Lisa replied, "We've convinced our manager that this is the right way to go, so don't throw a wrench into it now." This is a prime example of "Résumé Driven Design," where technology is chosen because it will be nice to use and may improve the programmer's skill set. But blindly picking a framework for your project is like having kids to save on taxes. It just doesn't work.

Before even thinking about a new technology or framework, identify what problem you are trying to solve. How you even form the sentence makes a difference; if you say, "We need technology *xyzzy* because...," then the battle for common sense is already lost. You need to start off by saying, "It's too hard to..." or "It takes too long too..." or something similar. Now that you've identified a genuine problem that needs solving, consider the following:

Does it really solve the problem? OK, this may sound blindingly obvious, but does the technology actually solve the particular problem you're facing? Or, more pointedly, are you relying on marketing claims or secondhand advice to assess its capabilities? Make sure it does what you want without any deleterious side effects; write a small prototype if needed.

Will you be tied to this technology? Some technologies (particularly frameworks) are a one-way trip. Once you're committed to them, there's no turning back. That lack of *reversibility* (see [HT00]) can be fatal later on a project, when conditions have changed. Consider just how open or proprietary the technology is.

What about maintenance costs? Will it end up being more expensive to maintain this technology over time? After all, the solution shouldn't be more expensive than the problem, or you've made a bad investment. One project we know of spends $50,000 a year on a support contract for a rules engine—but the database has only thirty rules. That's pretty expensive overkill.

When you look at a potential framework (or any technology, really), you may be drawn to the various features it has to offer. Then you might find yourself justifying the use of the framework based on these additional features you found. But are those additional features really needed? It may be that you're finding problems to fit the solution you have discovered, much like an impulsive buyer at the checkout counter (which is exactly why they put that stuff there).

Not long ago Venkat came across a project where Brad, a consultant, had sold management on the use of a proprietary framework. Venkat saw that, while the framework was certainly interesting, it really couldn't be justified on the project.

However, management was convinced they wanted to move forward with it. Ever polite, Venkat backed out, not wanting to be a stumbling block to their progress. A year later, the project was nowhere near completion—they had spent months writing code to maintain the framework and modifying their code to fit within it.

Andy had a similar experience where his client wanted to take advantage of open source—all of it, apparently; they had a "new-technology stew" so thick that they never actually got all the pieces to even work together.

If you find yourself building something fancy (and in the process developing your own framework from scratch), then wake up and smell the smoke. The less code you write, the less you have to maintain.

Don't build what you can download

For instance, if you have a hankering to develop your own persistence layer, remember Ted Neward's remark that "object-relational mapping is the Vietnam of computer science." You can spend more time and effort building only what you need to build for your application—the domain or application-specific stuff.

Choose technology based on need. *Determine your needs first, and then evaluate the use of technologies for those specific problems. Ask critical questions about the use of any technology, and answer them genuinely.*

What It Feels Like

A new technology should feel like a new tool that does a better job; it shouldn't *become* your job.

Keeping Your Balance

- Maybe it's too early in the project to really evaluate your technical requirements. That's fine. Perhaps a simple hashtable can stand in for a database while you're prototyping and demoing with users. Don't rush to decide on a technology if you don't have enough experience to make the decision yet.

- Every technology has advantages and drawbacks. Whether it's open source or a commercial product, a framework, a tool, or a language, be aware of the trade-offs that come with it.

- Don't build what you can readily download. Building everything you need from the ground up may be necessary, but it is the most expensive and risky option.

13 ▶ Keep It Releasable

"We just found a showstopper that you need to fix right away.
Stop what you're doing, and go ahead and make the fix; don't
bother with the usual procedures. No need to tell anyone else
about it—just get going. Hurry."

It sounds innocent enough. A critical fix needs to be checked in. It's a small thing, and the need is urgent, so you agree to take care of it.

The fix goes smoothly. You check in the code and return to your original, high-priority task. Then the screaming begins. Too late, you realize that a fellow developer has checked in an incompatible change, and now you've rendered the system unusable for everyone. It's going to take a lot more work (and time) to get the system back to a releasable state. Now you're stuck! You'll have to tell everyone you can't deliver the fix as you promised. And the devil laughs, "Bwahahahaha!"

Now you're in a bad position: the system is unreleasable. You've suddenly created risk and created an opportunity for bad things to happen.

In 1836, General Antonio López de Santa Anna, then president of Mexico, charged his way through west Texas, sending General Sam Houston and his men on the retreat. When Santa Anna reached the banks of the Buffalo bayou (in southeast Texas), he ordered his troop to rest. The legend says that he was so confident he did not bother to post sentries. When General Houston finally decided to charge late that afternoon, Santa Anna's army did not even have the time to form up. They lost this decisive battle, changing Texas forever.[5]

Anytime you are unprepared is the perfect time for the enemy to strike. Think about it: how often does your application slip into a nonreleasable state? Does your code in the **Checked-in code is always ready for action** repository appear like Santa Anna's army on that fateful afternoon—not in formation and unable to execute at a moment's notice?

When working in a team, you have to be sensitive to the changes you make, constantly keeping in mind that you affect and influence the state of the system and the productivity of the whole team. You

[5]http://www.sanjacinto-museum.org/The_Battle/April_21st_1836

wouldn't tolerate someone littering the kitchen area at the office, so why would you tolerate someone trashing your project's code?

There's a simple workflow to follow to make sure you don't check in broken code:

Run your local tests. Begin by making sure the code you're working on compiles and passes all of its unit tests. Then make sure all of the other tests in the system pass as well.

Check out the latest source. Get the latest copy of the source code from the version control system, and compile and test against that. Very often, this is where a surprise will show up: someone else may have made a change that's incompatible with yours.

Check in. Now that you have the latest version of code compiling and passing its tests, you can check it in.

Now during that process, you may discover a problem—someone else may have checked in code that does not compile or pass its tests. When that happens, let them know right away—and possibly warn the rest of the team if need be. Or, even better, have your *continuous integration* system point it out automatically.

Now that might sound a bit intimidating, but it shouldn't. Continuous integration systems are simply applications that check out, build, and test your code constantly in the background. They are easy enough to cobble together yourself using scripts, but you get more features and stability with an existing free, open-source solution. You might want to take a look at Martin Fowler's article[6] or Mike Clark's book, *Pragmatic Project Automation: How to Build, Deploy, and Monitor Java Applications* [Cla04], for all the details.

Looking forward a bit, suppose you hear about an upcoming significant change that may break the system. Don't just let it happen—take the warning seriously, and explore ways you can avoid disrupting the system when the check-in happens. Consider options that will help you introduce and transition those changes smoothly so the system is available for continual testing and feedback as the development proceeds.

Although it's important to keep the application releasable, it's not always that easy. For instance, consider a change to the database

---

[6]http://www.martinfowler.com/articles/continuousIntegration.html

schema, an external file format, or a message format. Changes such as these often affect large parts of the application and can render it unusable until a significant amount of code is changed. However, you have options to ease that pain.

Version the database schema, the external files, and so on, as well as the APIs that reference it, so that all related changes can be tested. This versioning isolates your changes from the rest of the code base so other aspects of the application can continue to be developed and tested.

You can also branch the code in your version control system to address these issues (but branch with care; wild branching causes more problems than it solves. See *Pragmatic Version Control Using CVS* [TH03] and *Pragmatic Version Control Using Subversion* [Mas05] for details).

 Keep your project releasable at all times. *Ensure that the project is always compilable, runnable, tested, and ready to deploy at a moment's notice.*

What It Feels Like

You feel confident that anytime the boss, the chairman of the board, QA, a customer, or your spouse comes by the office to visit, you can show them the latest build of the software without hesitation. Your project is simply always in a ready-to-run, stable state.

Keeping Your Balance

- Sometimes you can't invest the time and energy needed to keep the system in a releasable state throughout a major set of changes. If it would take a month's effort just to keep the application available throughout a week's worth of changes, then go for the week of downtime. But this should be the exception, not the rule.

- If you must render the system unreleasable for an extended period, have a branched version (of code and schema) you can still continue to experiment with—and fall back on. Do not render the system unreleasable and irreversible as well.

Integrate Early, Integrate Often

"Don't waste time thinking about integrating your code until the very end of the development phase, or at least until development is well underway. After all, why bother integrating code unless it's done? You'll have plenty of time at the end of the project to integrate code."

As we've said, a main aspect of agility is continuous development, not episodic. That's especially necessary when it comes to integrating code you've written with code the rest of the team has been working on.

Most developers would like to postpone integration for several good reasons. Sometimes the mere thought of working with more code or another subsystem may be too much to bear right now. It's easy to think, "I'm already under pressure to get things done, and the last thing I need is more work and trouble with other people's code." We've also heard excuses such as "I do not have time for that" or "It's quite an effort to set that up on my machine, and I don't want to do that now."

But integration is one of the major risk areas in product development. As you let a subsystem grow, unintegrated, you're exposing yourself to greater and greater risk—the rest of the world is marching on without you, and the potential for divergence will just keep increasing. Instead, it's easier to address risks as early as you can, while the risk and the relative pain level remains fairly low. The longer you wait, the more painful it will be.

In Venkat's early years in Chennai, India, he used to catch a train to school. Like any big-city, rush-hour commuter in India, he invariably had to jump in and out of trains that were already in motion. Now, you can't just leap into a moving train from a standing position; there's a very painful lesson on the laws of physics to be learned there. Instead, you first start running alongside the train and then get hold of it while gaining momentum. Finally you make the leap onto the train.

Software integration is like that. If you continue developing your code in isolation and one day suddenly jump to integrate, don't be surprised at the beating you'll get. You've probably seen this happen on your projects, where the time toward the end of the development phase becomes very frustrating. People spend days and nights integrating.

You Can Integrate and Isolate

Integration and isolation are not mutually exclusive; you can integrate and isolate at the same time.

Use *mock objects* to isolate the code from its dependencies so you can test before you integrate. A mock object is a stand-in for the real object (or subsystem). Just as movie actors have a stand in to take their place while the crew fiddles with the lights, a mock object stands in for the real object: it doesn't offer the functionality of the real object, but it's easier to control and can simulate the desired behavior for testing more easily.

You can unit test your code in isolation using mock objects instead of immediately integrating and testing with the rest of the system; as soon as you have some confidence that it works, then you can integrate it.

The only positive aspect is the free pizza you enjoy while being stuck at the office.

There's a tension between the need to isolate and the need to integrate early. When you develop in isolation, you'll find development quicker and more productive, and you can nail down problems more effectively (see Practice 35, *Attack Problems in Isolation*, on page 139). But that doesn't mean you should avoid or delay integration (see the sidebar on the current page). You should generally integrate your code at least several times a day and probably never go longer than two to three days at most.

By integrating early, you get to see how subsystems interact and interoperate, and you get to evaluate how information is shared and communicated. The earlier you understand

Never accept big-bang integration

and address these issues, the less work you'll have to do fixing them. That's true for 3 developers on a 50,000-line code base, and for 5,000 developers on a 30-million-line code base. If instead you postpone integration, then these issues may turn into difficult tasks that require significant—and far-reaching—code changes, causing delays and general chaos.

Integrate early, integrate often. *Code integration is a major source of risk. To mitigate that risk, start integration early and continue to do it regularly.*

What It Feels Like

When you're doing it right, integration stops feeling like a separate, onerous task. It's just part of the regular code-writing cycle. The problems that arise are small and easily addressed.

Keeping Your Balance

- Successful integration means that all the unit tests continue to pass. As per the Hippocratic oath, "First, do no harm."

- Normally you want to integrate your code with the rest of the team multiple times per day, say at least five to ten times on an average day and maybe much more. But there is a point of diminishing returns if you integrate every single line of code every time you make a change. If you find yourself spending all your time going through the motions of integrating code instead of writing code, you're doing it too often.

- If you don't integrate often enough (say you integrate only once a day, once a week, or worse), you may find you're spending all your time working out problems caused by integrating code instead of writing code. If your integration problems are large, you're not integrating often enough.

- For prototypes and experimental code, you may want to work in isolation and not waste effort on integration. But don't stay isolated too long; once you learn from the experience, work toward integration quickly.

Automate Deployment Early

"It's OK to install your product manually, especially to QA. You don't have to do it all that often, and they are pretty good about copying all the right files."

It's nice that the application works on your machine and for your favorite developers and testers. But it needs to work well when deployed on users' machines as well. If it works on your development server, that's fine, but it needs to work in the production environment too.

This means you need to be able to deploy your application onto the target machines in a reliable and repeatable way. Unfortunately, most developers tend to ignore deployment issues until the end of the project. The result is that they often end up deploying with missing dependent components, missing image files, and improper directory structures.

If a developer changes the directory structure for the application, or gets creative and shares image directories between different applications, this might break the installation process. You want to find these kinds of problems quickly while the change is still fresh in everyone's minds. Finding them weeks or months later, especially when getting ready for an important off-site demo, is no fun.

If you currently install your application for QA manually, consider taking some time to automate the process. Do that, and you'll have the basis for a fully fledged end-user installation

> QA should test deployment

system ready to go. And by doing it early, you give your QA team a chance to test both your application and its installation procedures.[7] If instead you manually install the application for them, what happens when the application goes into production? You wouldn't want to run around installing the application on every user's machine or on every possible server in different locations, even if you do get paid overtime.

Having the automated deployment system in place also makes it easier to keep up with the changes in dependencies during the life of the

---

[7]Make sure they can easily tell what version of software they are running, to avoid confusion.

Andy Says...

Delivery from Day One

There are a lot of advantages to having full deployment immediately, instead of waiting for later in the project. In fact, some
projects even set up a full installation environment before Day
One of the project ever starts!

At the Pragmatic Programmers, we were asked to put together
a simple demo for a prospective client—a proof of concept, if
you will. Even though the project itself hadn't started yet, we
had unit tests, continuous integration, and a Windows-based
installer. This allowed us to deliver the demo simply and easily: all the client had to do was click a link from our website,
and they could install the demo themselves on a variety of
machines.

Being able to demonstrate that sort of capability even before
the contract is signed sends a powerful, professional message.

project. Perhaps you've forgotten to add a required library or component to the installation—running the automated installation on an arbitrary machine will identify what's missing quickly. If something is going
to break because of missing components or incompatible libraries, you
want those problems to surface sooner rather than later.

Deploy your application automatically from the start.
*Use that deployment to install the application on arbitrary
machines with different configurations to test dependencies. QA should test the deployment as well as your application.*

What It Feels Like

It should feel invisible. Installing and/or deploying your product should
be easy, reliable, and repeatable. It just happens.

Keeping Your Balance

- You may have certain prerequisites for your product: a certain version of Java or Ruby, external database, or OS. If it makes a difference—and would result in a tech support call—check for necessary dependencies as part of the install process.

- Installers should never destroy user data without asking the user's permission.

- Deploying an emergency bug fix should be easy, especially in a production server environment. You know it will happen, and you don't want to have to do it manually, under pressure, at 3:30 a.m.

- The user should always to be able to remove an installation safely and completely—especially in a QA environment.

- If maintaining the install script is getting harder, that may be an early warning sign of support costs (and/or bad design decisions).

- When you combine your continuous integration system and a production CD or DVD burner, you can automatically produce a complete, labeled disc of your software with each build. Anyone who wants the latest build can just take the disc from the top of the pile and install it.

Get Frequent Feedback Using Demos

"It's not your fault; the problem lies with our customers—those pesky end users and clients. They always come up with so many changes, way past the deadline. They should just figure out what they want once and for all and then give us requirements so we can implement the system to their satisfaction. That's how it ought to work."

Requirements are as fluid as ink

Oftentimes you might hear that people want to "freeze" requirements.[8] It turns out that real-world requirements are as fluid as ink itself. You can't freeze requirements any more than you can freeze markets, competition, learning, evolution, or growth. And even if you tried, you'd almost certainly freeze the wrong ones. If you mistakenly expect your customers to give you solid, well-defined requirements before the start of your project, be prepared for major disappointment.

Nobody's minds or perspectives are frozen in time, especially not your project's customers. Even after they tell you what they want, their ideas and their expectations continue to evolve—especially once they begin to use portions of the new system and start to realize its impact and possibilities. That's just human nature.

As humans, we get better at what we do—whatever that is—slowly and incrementally. So your customers, after giving you the requirements, will be constantly figuring out ways to get better at using the features they asked you to implement. If all you do is take their initial requirements and implement them, you will certainly not be anywhere close to satisfying their requirements by the time of delivery—the requirements will have changed. You're exposing yourself to one of the biggest risks in software development: you've produced what they asked for, not what they've come to want. The result? Surprise, shock, and disappointment, instead of satisfaction.

Years ago in a numerical analysis course, Venkat was asked to simulate the trajectory of a spacecraft using some partial differential equations.

---

[8]Edward V. Berard noted, "Walking on water and developing software from a specification are easy if both are frozen."

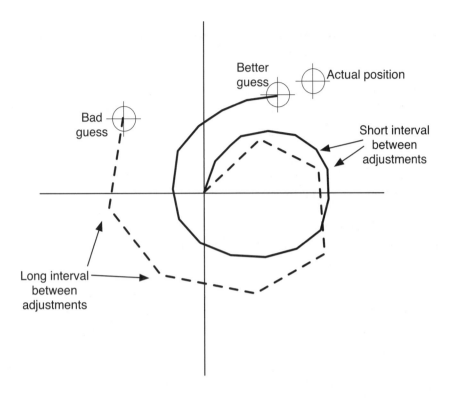

Figure 4.1: COMPUTED TRAJECTORY OF A SPACECRAFT

The program worked by figuring out the position at time $t+\delta$ based on the position at time t. The program's plotted trajectory looked something like the dashed line shown in Figure 4.1.

Notice the estimated position of the spacecraft was a long way away from where it was in reality; gravitational effects on the spacecraft's velocity did not just happen at each of the positions we decided to calculate. Instead, the effects of gravity happened all the time; it was continuous, rather than discrete. By ignoring the effects between the points, we kept adding errors to the calculation, and our spacecraft ended up in the wrong place.

Reducing the iteration interval (the value of δ) and running the calculations again reduced the overall error. This time the estimated position (shown by the solid line) was much closer to the actual position.

Imagine your customer's expectations are like the actual position of the spacecraft. Your success in software development is based on how close you end up to your customer's expectations. The discrete positions you calculate are opportunities to show the customer what you have done so far. These are the times when you get their input and feedback. This feedback then changes the direction you take when you set off on the next leg of the journey.

It's pretty easy to see that the larger the gap between when you get their requirements and the time you show them what you've done, the further off course you'll be.

At regular, consistent intervals, such as at the end of an iteration, meet with your customers, and demonstrate the features and functionality you've completed so far.

If you consult with your customers frequently, getting their input as you develop, everyone benefits. Your customers are more aware of the progress you're making. As a result, they are able to refine the requirements, first in their minds and then, by giving feedback, in yours. They are able to steer you based on their evolving understanding and expectations, and you are able to program closer to their actual needs. The customer can prioritize the tasks in the context of the progress you've made and the available time and budget.

Is there downside to seeking frequent feedback in shorter iteration cycles? In the spacecraft trajectory program, it took longer for the program to run when δ was decreased. You may be wondering if using shorter iterations will slow things down and delay your project.

Think of it this way: imagine getting all the way to the end of a two-year project only to realize that you and your customer had a fundamental disconnect when it came to a key requirement. You thought back orders were handled one way, but your customer meant something totally different. Now, two years later, you've produced a system that's a million lines of code away from the one the customer wanted. Undoing a goodly portion of two years worth of effort is going to be expensive, to say the least.

Instead, imagine you had shown them demonstrations of the system as you went along. Two months into the project they say, "Wait a minute; that's not what a back order is supposed to do." This triggers a panic

Andy Says...

Keep a Project Glossary

Inconsistent terminology is a major cause of requirements mis-understandings. Businesses have a tendency to attach very specific, important meaning to what appears to be common, innocent-sounding words.

I've seen this happen quite often: programmers on the team will use different terminology than the users or businesspeople, and the resulting "impedance mismatch" causes bugs and design errors.

To avoid these sorts of issues, keep a *project glossary*. It should be publicly accessible, perhaps on an intranet website or Wiki. It almost sounds trivial—it's just a list of terms and their definitions. But it helps to make sure you are actually communicating with the users.

Throughout the project, choose appropriate names for program constructs—classes, methods, modules, variables, and so on—from the glossary, and check to make sure the definitions continue to match the users' expectations.

meeting: you review the requirements and assess the changes needed. It's a small price to pay to avoid a disaster.

Get feedback often. If your iteration cycle is quarterly or annually (which is too long), reduce it to weekly or biweekly. Proactively get customer feedback on the features and functionality you are implementing.

Develop in plain sight. *Keep your application in sight (and in the customers' mind) during development. Bring customers together and proactively seek their feedback using demos every week or two.*

What It Feels Like

After some start-up period, you should settle into a comfortable groove where the team and the customer enjoy a healthy, creative relationship.

Track Issues

As the project progresses, you'll get a lot of feedback—corrections, suggestions, change requests, feature enhancement, bug fixes, and so on. That's a lot of information to keep track of. Random emails or scribbled sticky notes don't cut it. Instead, log all this material into a tracking system, perhaps using a web interface. See *Ship It!* (RG05) for details.

Surprises should become rare, and the customer should feel they have an appropriate level of control over the direction of the project.

Keeping Your Balance

- When you first propose this method of working with the customer, they may balk at the thought of so many "releases." It's important that they understand these are *internal* releases (demos) for their own benefit and aren't necessarily targeted for distribution to the entire user community.

- Some clients may feel that daily, weekly, or even biweekly sessions are too much for them to handle. After all, they already have full-time jobs.

  Be respectful of their time. If the customer is comfortable with only monthly sessions, then monthly it is.

- Some customer's staff may be assigned to participate in your demo sessions *as* their full-time job. They'd like nothing better than hourly feedback and demos. While that may work out great, you might find that's too much for you to handle and still produce any code for them to see! Scale it back so that you meet when you're really done and have something to show.

- The demo is intended for customers to give you feedback and help steer the project. It is *not* supposed to agitate or annoy them because of lack of functionality or stability. If it's not stable, don't show it. Set the expectations about functionality early and clearly: let the customers know that they are looking at an application under development, not a final, finished product.

17 ▶ Use Short Iterations, Release in Increments

"We've got this beautiful project plan with all the tasks and deliverables scheduled for the next three years. When we release the product then, we'll capture the market!"

The Unified Process and the agile methodologies both prescribe *iterative* and *incremental* development.[9] With *incremental* development, you develop application functionality in several small groups at a time. Each round of development builds on the functionality of the previous one and adds features that enhance the product's value. You can *release* or demo the product at that point.

Iterative development is where you carry out the various tasks of development—analysis, design, implementation, testing, and seeking feedback—in small, repetitive cycles, called *iterations*.

The end of an iteration marks a milestone. However, the product may or may not be available at that time for real use. An increment of the product is complete when, at the end of an iteration, you are ready to release it for real use, along with resources to support, train, and maintain. Each increment generally includes many iterations.

According to Capers Jones, "...Large system development is a very hazardous undertaking." Large projects are more likely to fail. They generally do not follow an iterative and incremental development plan, or the length of the iterations is too long. (For a good dis-

> Show me a detailed long-term plan, and I'll show you a project that's doomed

cussion on iterative and evolutionary development, and *evidence* of its correlation to risk, productivity, and defects, refer to *Agile and Iterative Development: A Manager's Guide* [Lar04].) Larman argues that software development is not predictive manufacturing but inventive in nature. A project that is scheduled years before a customer puts the application to real use is most certainly doomed.

---

[9]But then again, *all* diet plans suggest you should eat less and exercise more. But each plan's advice on how to *achieve* those goals varies widely.

The idea of tackling a large project by taking small steps is key to an agile approach. Large leaps increase your risk; small steps help you maintain your balance.

You can find many examples of iterative and incremental development around you. Consider the XML specifications from the World Wide Web Consortium: Document Type Definitions (DTDs), which define the structure and vocabulary of XML documents, were released as part of the original specification. Although DTDs solved the issues at the time of their design, actual usage brought to light a number of limitations and problems. Based on user feedback and further understanding, more effective second-generation solutions for defining document structures, such as Schema, were created. Had they waited to come up with something superior to start with, we might not have seen XML become dominant—we got experience and insight by releasing early.

Most users would rather have good software today than wait for superior software a year later (see "Good Enough Software" in *The Pragmatic Programmer: From Journeyman to Master* [HT00]). Identify core features that'll make the product usable, and get them into production—into the hands of the real users—as soon as possible.

Depending on the nature of the product, releasing an increment may take weeks, or perhaps months. But if you're looking at delivering in a year or two, you should reevaluate and replan. You may argue that building complex software takes time and that you can't produce a large software application incrementally. If that's the case, then don't produce one large application! Build it in smaller, useful pieces—that is, follow incremental development. Even NASA used iterative and incremental development to create the complex software for its space shuttle (See *Design, Development, Integration: Space Shuttle Primary Flight Software System* [MR84]).

Ask the users what features are essential to make the product usable. Don't be distracted by all the nice features you might possibly have, and don't aim for the most glamorous user interface you can envision.

You want to get an application into users' hands quickly for a number of reasons: by getting it into the hands of users, you generate revenue, and it's easier to legitimize the efforts to continue funding the product. Feedback from the users helps us understand what they really care about and what should be written next. You may learn that some fea-

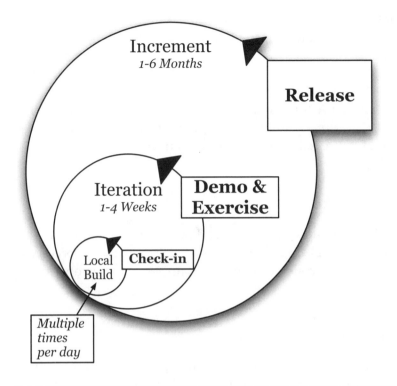

Figure 4.2: NESTED AGILE DEVELOPMENT CYCLES

tures you thought were important are not anymore—we all know how volatile the marketplace is. Release your application soon, because it might not even be relevant later.

Having short iterations and smaller increments helps developers stay focused. If you are told you have a year to complete a project, in your mind you see something a long time off. It is hard to have the drive needed to focus when something is so far away. Our society prizes instant gratification—we want results quickly, and we like seeing things take shape sooner than later. That isn't necessarily bad; it is actually good if it can be turned into productivity and positive feedback.

Figure 4.2 shows the relationship between the major cycles in an agile project. The ideal duration for each increment is a few weeks to a few months, depending on the size of the project. Within the development cycle for each increment, you should use short iterations (no longer than a couple of weeks). End each iteration with a demo, and place a working copy of the product in the hands of select customers who will provide feedback.

Develop in increments. *Release your product with minimal, yet usable, chunks of functionality. Within the development of each increment, use an iterative cycle of one to four weeks or so.*

What It Feels Like

A short iteration feels sharply focused and productive. You have a solid, well-defined goal in sight, and you meet it. A firm deadline forces you to make the hard decisions, and no issues are left open or unresolved for very long.

Keeping Your Balance

- Determining an appropriate iteration length is a critical question of balance. Andy had a client who firmly believed that iterations should be exactly four weeks in length, because that's what they had read. But the team was dying at that pace; they couldn't develop the code *and* tend to their ongoing maintenance responsibilities. The solution was to use a four-week iteration separated by one week of maintenance work and then begin the next iteration. There's no rule that iterations have to be back to back.

- If there's not enough time in each iteration, then the tasks are too large or the iteration is too short (on average; don't change just one iteration because of oddball circumstances). Feel the rhythm.

- If there is a disconnect between the users' needs and the features of the release, then perhaps the iteration was too long. As users' needs, technology, and our understanding of the requirements change over time, those changes need to be reflected in the release. If you find yourself still working on old notions and stale ideas, then perhaps you waited too long to make adjustments.

- An incremental release must be usable and provide value to customers. How do you know what they'll find valuable? Ask them.

18 ▶ # Fixed Prices Are Broken Promises

"We have to deliver a fixed bid for this project. We don't have all the details yet but need to put a bid in. I need an estimate for the whole team by Monday, and we'll have to deliver the whole project by the end of the year."

Fixed-price contracts present a problem to an agile team. We've been talking all along about working in a continuous, iterative, and incremental fashion, and now someone comes along and wants to know ahead of time how long it will take and how much it will cost.

From the customer's point of view, this is all perfectly reasonable. They work like this to get buildings built, parking lots paved, and so on. Why can't software be more like an established industry—say, building construction?

Maybe it's actually a *lot* like building construction—real building construction, not our image of building construction. According to a 1998 study in the United Kingdom, some 30% of the cost of construction projects came from rework due to errors.[10] This wasn't because of changes in requirements, or changes in the laws of physics, but simple errors. Cutting a beam too short. Making the hole for the window too large. Simple, familiar mistakes.

A software project is subject to all the simple mistakes plus fundamental changes to the requirements (no, not a shed, I want a skyscraper!), huge variability in individual and team performance (20X or more, depending on whose studies you believe), and of course, the constant inrush of new technology (from now on, the nails are circular).

Given the inherent volatility and irreproducibility of software projects, coming up with a fixed price ahead of time pretty much guarantees a broken promise in the works. What alternatives do we have? Can we get better at estimation or maybe negotiate a different sort of a deal?

> A fixed price guarantees a broken promise

---

[10]*Rethinking Construction: The Report of the Construction Task Force*, Department for Transport Local Government and the Regions, 01 Jan 1998, Office of the Deputy Prime Minister, London, England

Depending on your environment, you may be able to do either. If you absolutely, positively have to provide a price up front (for a government contract, say), then you may want to investigate some heavy-duty estimation techniques such as COCOMO or Function Point analysis. But these aren't particularly agile techniques, and they don't come for free. If the project is substantially similar to other projects you've done with this same team, you're certainly in better shape: developing a simple website for one customer will be pretty much the same as the next.

But many projects aren't like that. Most projects involve business applications that vary tremendously from one client to the next. The projects of discovery and invention need to be treated much more collaboratively. Perhaps you can offer a slightly different arrangement. Try proposing the following steps:

1. Offer to build an initial, small, useful portion of the system (in the construction analogy, perhaps just the garage). Pick a small enough set of features such that this first delivery should take no more than six to eight weeks. Explain that not all the features will make it in but that enough will be delivered so that the users could actually be productive.

2. At the end of that first iteration, the client has two choices: they can agree to continue to the next iteration, with the next set of features; or, they can cancel your contract, pay you only for the few weeks worth of work you've done, and either throw it away or get some other group to take it and run with it.

3. If they go ahead, you're in a better position to forecast what you can get done during the next iteration. At the end of the next iteration, the client still has those same two choices: stop now, or go on to the next.

The advantage to the client is that the project doesn't "go dark." They get to see progress (or lack of it) early on. They are always in control and can pull the plug at any time, with no contractual penalty. They are in control of what features go in first and exactly how much money they are spending. Overall, the client is facing much less risk.

And you're doing iterative and incremental development.

Estimate based on real work. *Let the team actually work on the current project, with the current client, to get realistic estimates. Give the client control over their features and budget.*

What It Feels Like

Your estimates will change throughout the project—they aren't fixed. But you'll feel increasingly confident that you can forecast the amount accomplished with each iteration better and better. Your estimates improve over time.

Keeping Your Balance

- If you aren't comfortable with the answer, see if you can change the question.

- If you are developing in a plan-based, nonagile environment, then you might want to consider either a plan-based, nonagile development methodology or a different environment.

- If you refuse to give any estimation before finishing a first iteration, you may lose the contract to someone else who gives an estimate, however unrealistic their promise may be.

- Being agile doesn't mean "Just start coding, and we'll eventually know when we're done." You still need to give a ballpark estimate, with an explanation of how you arrived at it and the margin of error given your current knowledge and assumptions.

- If you're in a position where none of this is an option and you simple *have* to work to a fixed price, you need to develop really good estimation skills.

- You might also consider a fixed price per iteration set in the contract while leaving the number of iterations loose, perhaps determined by ongoing work orders (a.k.a. "Statement of Work").

*One test is worth a thousand expert
opinions.*

▶ Bill Nye, The Science Guy

Chapter 5

Agile Feedback

In an agile project, we're always seeking feedback in order to make many small, continuous adjustments. But where does all this feedback come from?

In the previous chapter, we talked about working closely with users—getting good feedback from them and acting on it. In this chapter, we'll talk primarily about getting feedback in other ways. As Bill Nye observes, tests of any sort are definitive; we'll implement that idea to ensure that you always *know* the state of your project's health and don't have to guess.

Many projects get into trouble when the code base gets out of hand. Bug fixes beget more bugs, which beget more bug fixes, and the whole pile of cards comes crashing down. What we need is a constant monitor—a constant source of feedback to make sure the code base hasn't deteriorated and continues to work at least as well as it did yesterday, if not even better. We'll see how to *Put Angels on Your Shoulders* to watch out for your code starting on page 81.

But that won't stop you from designing an interface or an API that's cumbersome or hard to use correctly. For that, you'll need to *Use It Before You Build It* (which starts on page 85).

But of course, just because it works for one unit test on your machine doesn't automatically mean it will work the same on any other machine. See why *Different Makes a Difference*, starting on page 90.

Now that you have decent APIs and clean code, it might be a good idea to ensure that code actually produces the results the users expect. You can *Automate Acceptance Testing* to make sure the code is correct—and stays that way. We'll take a look at that on page 93.

Everyone wants to see progress on a project, but it's easy to go astray by watching misleading indicators or to fall prey to the false authority of a pretty Gantt or PERT chart or a nice calendaring tool. Instead, you want to *Measure Real Progress*, and we'll show you how on page 96.

Although we talked about working with users to get feedback during development, there's another time—long after the product has been released—when you need to once again *Listen to Users*, and we'll explain starting on page 99.

19 ▶ Put Angels on Your Shoulders

"You can't justify the time and effort it takes to write unit tests. It will just delay the project. You're a darn good programmer anyway—unit tests are just a waste of time, and we're already in a crunch."

Code changes rapidly. Every time your finger hits the keyboard, the code has changed. Agility is all about managing change, and the code is the one thing that probably changes the most.

To cope with that, you need constant feedback about the health of the code: does it do what you intend? Did that last change break anything unexpectedly? What you need is the equivalent of an angel looking over your shoulder, constantly making sure everything is OK. To do that, you need automated unit tests.

Now, some developers are put off by the idea of unit testing; after all, it has that *testing* word in it, and surely that's somebody else's job. Just ignore the name for now, and consider this to be an excellent coding feedback technique.

Coding feedback

Think how most developers have typically worked with code in the past: you write a little code and then stick in a few print statements to see the value of a few key variables. You run the code, maybe from a debugger or maybe from a few lines of a stub program. You look at the results manually, fix any problems that come up, then throw the stub program away or exit the debugger, and move on to the next item.

Agile-style unit testing takes that same, familiar process and kicks it up a notch. Instead of throwing the stub code away, you save it, and continue to run it automatically. Instead of manually inspecting the interesting variables, you write code to check for specific values.

Since the code to test a variable for a specific value (and keep track of how many tests you ran, and so on) is pretty common, you can use standard frameworks to help with the low-level housekeeping of writing and organizing tests. There's JUnit for Java, NUnit for C#/.NET, HttpUnit for testing web servers, and so on. In fact, there's an *x*Unit framework for just about every language and environment you can imagine. Most of these are listed at and available from
`http://xprogramming.com/software.htm`.

Be Sure of What You're Testing

Reader David Bock shares the following story with us:

"I was recently working on a module of a much larger project, converting the build from Ant to Maven. This was solid, well-tested code that was in use in production. I was working away, late into the evening, and everything was going well. I changed part of the build process, and all of a sudden, I had a failing unit test. I spent some time trying to figure out why my change would make a test fail but eventually gave up and rolled it back. The test still failed. I went digging into the test, and I found that the failure was in a test on a utility for calculating times; specifically, it was returning an instance of Date set to noon tomorrow. I looked at the test and found that it was taking the time of the test execution and using that as a parameter to the test. The method had a stupid off-by-one error so that if you called the method between 11 p.m. and midnight, it would actually return noon of the *same day*, not tomorrow."

Important lessons from this story:

- Make sure your tests are repeatable. Using the current date or time as a parameter makes the test sensitive to the time it is run, using the IP address of your machine makes it sensitive to which machine it's run on, and so on.

- Test your boundary conditions. 11:59:59 and 0:00:00 are good choices for time.

- Never allow failing tests. In the previous case, one test was failing all the time, but because there were two dozen failing tests that went up or down by a few every day naturally, no one noticed the one pseudo-random failure.

Once you have a few unit tests, automate them. That is, run the unit tests on your code every time you compile or build. Think of the results of the unit test as being equivalent to the compiler itself—if the code doesn't pass its unit tests (or doesn't *have* unit tests), it's just as bad as if it didn't compile.

Next, arrange for a *build machine* to sit in the background, constantly getting the latest version of your source code, compiling it, running the unit tests, and letting you know immediately if anything has gone awry.

The combination of local unit tests, run with every compilation, and the continuous build machine compiling and running the unit tests, creates the angel on your shoulder. If something breaks you'll know about it right away—when it's easiest (and cheapest) to fix.

With unit tests in place, acting as regression tests, you're now free to refactor the code base at will. You can rewrite and redesign code and experiment as needed: the unit tests will ensure that you haven't broken anything accidentally. That's a very powerful freedom; you don't have to code as if "walking on eggshells."

Unit testing is one of the more popular agile practices, and as a result, a lot of books and other materials can help you get started. If you're new to the idea, take a look at *Pragmatic Unit Testing* (in both Java [HT03] and C# [HT04] versions). For a more in-depth, recipe-based approach, check out *JUnit Recipes* [Rai04].

To hook up automation for unit tests (and a number of other useful things), see *Pragmatic Project Automation: How to Build, Deploy, and Monitor Java Applications* [Cla04]. Although it's focused primarily on Java, equivalent tools exist for .NET and other environments.

If you're still looking for reasons to get started with unit testing, here are just a few:

Unit testing provides instant feedback. Your code gets exercised repeatedly. As you change and rewrite your code, the test cases will check that you haven't broken any existing contract. You can quickly identify and fix any problems.

Unit testing makes your code robust. Testing helps you think through the behavior of the code, exercising the positive, negative, and exceptional cases.

Unit testing can be a helpful design tool. As we'll see in Practice 20, *Use It Before You Build It*, on page 85, unit testing can help you achieve a pragmatic and simpler design.

Unit testing is a confidence booster. You've tested your code and exercised its behavior for a variety of different conditions; this will give you confidence when faced with new, high pressure tasks on tight deadlines.

Unit tests can act as probes when solving problems. Unit tests act like the oscilloscope probes you'd use to test printed circuit boards. You can quickly take a pulse of the inner workings of the code when a problem arises. This gives you a natural way to pinpoint and solve problems (see Practice 35, *Attack Problems in Isolation*, on page 139).

Unit tests are reliable documentation. When you start learning a new API, any unit tests for it can serve as accurate, reliable documentation.

Unit tests are a learning aid. As you begin to use a new API, you can start by writing tests against that API to facilitate your learning. These learning tests not only help you understand the behavior of the API but also help you quickly find any incompatible changes that might be introduced later.

> **Use automated unit tests.** *Good unit tests warn you about problems immediately. Don't make any design or code changes without solid unit tests in place.*

What It Feels Like

You rely on having unit tests. Code without tests makes you feel uncomfortable as if you were teetering on a high wire without a net.

Keeping Your Balance

- Unit testing is an investment. Invest wisely. Testing accessors or trivial methods is probably not time well spent.

- Many of the excuses people use to avoid unit testing really point to design flaws in the code. Usually, the louder the protest, the worse the design.

- Unit testing is only as effective as your test coverage. You might want to look at using test coverage tools to give you a rough idea of where you stand.

- More tests don't automatically mean better quality: tests have to be effective. If tests never catch anything, maybe they aren't testing the right things.

Use It Before You Build It

"Go ahead and complete all of your library code. There's plenty of time later to see what people think of it. Just throw the code over the wall for now. I'm sure it's fine."

Many successful companies live by the slogan "Eat your own dog food." In other words, to make your product the best it can be, you need to actively use it yourself.

Fortunately, we're not in the dog-food business. But we are in the business of creating and calling APIs and using interfaces. That means you need to actually use your own interface before foisting it on the rest of the world. In fact, you need to use the interface that you're designing before you even implement the code behind it. How is that possible?

Using the technique known as *Test Driven Development* (TDD), you write code only after writing a failing unit test for that code. The test always comes first. Usually, the test case **Write tests before writing code** fails either because the code under test doesn't yet exist or because it doesn't yet contain the necessary logic to allow the test to pass.

By writing the tests first, you're looking at your code from the perspective of a user of the code, not of the implementer. And that makes a big difference; you'll find that you can design more usable, consistent interfaces because you have to use them yourself.

In addition, writing tests before writing code helps eliminate overly complicated designs and lets you focus on really getting the job done. Consider the following example of writing a program that allows two users to play tic-tac-toe.

As you start to think about designing code for the game, you might think of classes such as TicTacToeBoard, Cell, Row, Column, Player, User, Peg, Score, and Rules. Let's start with the TicTacToeBoard class, which represents the tic-tac-toe board itself (in terms of the core game logic, not the UI).

Here's a possible first test for the TicTacToeBoard class, written in C# using the NUnit test framework. It creates a board and asserts that the game is not already finished.

```
[TestFixture]
public class TicTacToeTest
{
  private TicTacToeBoard board;
  [SetUp]
  public void CreateBoard()
  {
    board = new TicTacToeBoard();
  }
  [Test]
  public void TestCreateBoard()
  {
    Assert.IsNotNull(board);
    Assert.IsFalse(board.GameOver);
  }
}
```

The test fails because the class TicTacToeBoard doesn't exist—you'll get a compilation error. You'd be pretty surprised if it passed, wouldn't you? That can happen—not often, but it does happen. Always make sure your tests fail before they pass in order to flush out potential bugs in the test. Let's implement that class:

```
public class TicTacToeBoard {
  public bool GameOver {
    get {
      return false;
    }
  }
}
```

In the GameOver property we'll return false for now. In general, you want to write the least code necessary to get the test to pass. This is a kind of lie—you know that the code is incomplete. But that doesn't matter, because later tests will force you to come back and add functionality.

What's the next step? First you have to decide who's going to start, so let's set up the first player. We'll start with a test for setting the first player:

```
[Test]
public void TestSetFirstPlayer() {
                  // what should go here?
}
```

At this point, the test is forcing you to make a decision. Before you can finish it, you have to decide how you're going to represent players in the code and how to assign them to the board. Here's one idea:

```
board.SetFirstPlayer(new Player("Mark"), "X");
```

This tells the board that the player Mark will be using the peg *X*.

While this will certainly work, do you really need the Player class or the first player's name? Perhaps, later, you might need to keep track of who the winner is. But that's not an issue right now. The YAGNI[1] (You Aren't Gonna Need It) principle says that you should not implement a feature until something needs it. At this point, there is no force that indicates you need the Player class.

Remember, we haven't written the SetFirstPlayer() method in the TicTac-ToeBoard class and we haven't written the Player class. We're still just trying to write a test. So let's assume the following code to set the first player:

```
board.SetFirstPlayer("X");
```

This conveys the notion that the first player's peg is *X*. It's also simpler than the first version. However, this version has an implicit risk: passing in an arbitrary character to SetFirstPlayer() means you'll have to add code that checks whether the parameter is either *O* or *X*, and you'll need to work out what to do when it isn't. So let's simplify even further. We'll have a simple flag to say whether the first player is an *O* or an *X*. Knowing that, we can now write our unit test:

```
[Test]
public void TestSetFirstPlayer() {
  board.FirstPlayerPegIsX = true;
  Assert.IsTrue(board.FirstPlayerPegIsX);
}
```

We can write the FirstPlayerPegIsX() as a **boolean** property and set it to the desired value. This looks simple and easy to use as well—much easier than dealing with the complexity of using the Player class. Once the test is written, you can get it to pass by implementing the FirstPlayerPegIsX property in the TicTacToeBoard class.

See how we started out by having a whole Player class and ended up simply using a **boolean** value? This simplification came about by testing *first*, before writing the underlying code.

---

[1]Coined by Ron Jeffries

Now remember, the point isn't to throw out good design practices and code everything as a large set of booleans! The point is to figure out what is the *minimum* amount of effort required to implement a given feature successfully. Overall, we programmers tend to err so much in the other direction—needlessly overcomplicating things—that it's very useful to try to err in the other direction.

It's easy to simplify code by eliminating classes that you haven't written yet. By contrast, once you have written code, you may feel compelled to keep that code and continue working with it (even if it's long past its expiration date).

Good design doesn't mean more classes

When you design and develop object-oriented systems, you probably feel compelled to use objects. There's a tendency to think that OO systems should be made of objects, and we sometimes force ourselves to create more and more classes of objects—whether they are really needed or not. Adding gratuitous code is always a bad idea.

TDD makes you go through the exercise of thinking about how you'll use the code before you get a chance to write it (or at least before you go too far into the implementation). This forces you to think about usability and convenience and lets you arrive at a more pragmatic design.

And of course, design isn't finished right at the beginning. You will continuously add tests, add code, and redesign the class over its lifetime (see Practice 28, *Code in Increments*, on page 116, for more on this basic idea).

Use it before you build it. *Use Test Driven Development as a design tool. It will lead you to a more pragmatic and simpler design.*

What It Feels Like

It feels like you always have a concrete reason to write code. You can concentrate on designing an interface without being overly distracted by implementation details.

Keeping Your Balance

- Don't get hung up on Test First vs. Test Before Checking Code In. Test First improves design, but you always have to Test Before Checking Code In.

- Every design can be improved.

- Unit tests may not be appropriate when you're experimenting with an idea or prototyping. In the unfortunate case that the code does move forward into a real system, you'll have to add the tests (but it's almost always better to start over from scratch).

- Unit tests alone don't guarantee a better design, but they make it easier to create one.

21   Different Makes a Difference

"As long as the code works on your machine, that's OK. Who cares if it works on some other platform? You don't have one."

When a vendor or a co-worker says those immortal words, "Oh, that won't make a difference," you can bet they are wrong. If something is different, odds are it *will* make a difference.

Venkat learned this lesson the hard way on a project. A colleague complained that Venkat's code was failing. But oddly, the situation was the same as one of the test cases that passed on Venkat's machine. It worked on one machine but not on the other.

They finally figured out the culprit was a difference in behavior of a .NET API on different platforms: Windows XP versus Windows 2003.[2] The platform was different—and it made a difference.

They were lucky to discover this problem by accident; otherwise, it may have been noticed only once the product shipped. Discovering such problems late can be very expensive—imagine releasing an application and only then finding out it breaks on one of the platforms you're supposed to be supporting.

You might ask your QA team to test your application on all supported platforms. But that may not be the most reliable tack if they're testing manually. We need a more developer-oriented approach!

You're already writing unit tests to exercise your code. Whenever you modify or refactor your code, you exercise your test cases before you check in the code. All you have to do now is exercise your test cases on each supported platform or environment.

If your application is expected to run on different operating systems (MacOS, Linux, Windows, etc.) or even on different versions of the same operating system (Windows 2000, Windows XP, Windows 2003, etc.), you need to test on all of them. If you expect your application to work on different versions of the Java Virtual Machine (VM) or .NET common language runtime (CLR), you need to test that as well.

---

[2]See Gotcha #74 in *.NET Gotchas* [Sub05].

Andy Says...

But It Works on My Machine...

I once had a client who needed better performance from their OS/2 system, so one of the bolder developers decided to rewrite the OS/2 operating system scheduler from scratch, in assembly language.

And it actually worked. Sort of. It worked really well on the original developer's machine, but they couldn't get it to work on any other machine. They even went so far as to purchase identical hardware from the same vendor and load up the same version of operating system, database, and other tools. No luck at all.

They tried facing the machines in the same direction, at the same time of day, with a sacrificial chicken for luck (OK, I'm making that part up, but the rest is true).

The team eventually abandoned the attempt. Messing with the undocumented internals of the operating system is most likely a fragile technique, not an agile one.

Automate to save time

But you probably already feel pressed for time, so how can you possibly take time to run tests on multiple platforms as well? Continuous integration[3] to the rescue!

As we saw in *Keep It Releasable* a continuous integration tool periodically fetches the code from your source control system and exercises it. If any test fails, it notifies the relevant developers. The notification may be through email, a pager, an RSS feed, or other more creative approaches.

To test on multiple platforms, you simply set up a continuous integration system on each. When you or a fellow developer checks in the code, the tests will be run automatically on each of these platforms. Imagine being informed of any failures on any platform within minutes of checking in your code! That's using your resources wisely.

---

[3]Read the seminal article entitled "Continuous Integration" by Martin Fowler at `http://www.martinfowler.com/articles/continuousIntegration.html`.

Hardware for build machines costs the equivalent of only a few hours of developer time. If needed, you can reduce the hardware cost even further by using products such as VMware or Virtual PC to run different versions of operating system, VM, or CLR on a single box.

Different makes a difference. Run unit tests on each supported platform and environment combination, using continuous integration tools. Actively find problems before they find you.

What It Feels Like

It feels like unit testing, only more so—it's unit testing across multiple worlds.

Keeping Your Balance

- Hardware is cheaper than developer time. But if you have a large number of supported platforms and configurations, you may need to be selective as to which ones you actively test in-house.

- Bugs that exist on all platforms may be spotted only because of stack layout differences, word-endian differences, etc., so even if you have fewer clients on Solaris than Linux, you still want to test on both.

- You don't want to be bombarded with five notifications for one error (that's like double taxation and contributes to "email fatigue"). Either lower the frequency of the integration build on all but one main platform/configuration to give you enough time to fix the main build if it breaks or roll up the errors in a single convenient report.

22 ▶ Automate Acceptance Testing

"All right, so your unit tests verify your code does what you think it should. Ship it. We'll find out if it's what the customers want soon enough."

You've worked with the users to develop the features they want, but now you need to make sure the data they're getting is correct—or at least correct from their point of view.

Andy was on a project a few years ago where their industry standard considered 12 a.m. as the last minute of the day, and 12:01 a.m. as the first minute of the new day (typically, business and computer systems consider 11:59 p.m. as the last minute of the day and 12 a.m. as the beginning of a new day). That small detail made a huge difference when it came to acceptance testing—things just wouldn't add up otherwise.

Critical business logic needs to be tested independent of the rest of the application, and the users need to approve the results.

But you don't want to drag the users in to check your results with every unit test. Instead, you want to automate the comparison of your customers' expectations with your actual implementation.

One wrinkle makes these sorts of acceptance tests different from usual unit tests. You'd like the users to be able to add, update, and modify their data as needed, without having to learn to write code. You have a couple of ways to go about that.

Andy has used a number of schemes that relied on data in flat files that users could edit directly. Venkat recently did something similar using an Excel spreadsheet. Depending on your environment, you may have something that's already a natural fit with your users (be it data in a flat file, an Excel spreadsheet, a database, or another form). Or, you might consider an existing tool that does most of this for you already.

FIT,[4] the Framework for Integrated Testing, is a helpful technology that makes it easier to use HTML tables as a mechanism to define and compare test cases and values.

---

[4] http://fit.c2.com.

Venkat Says...

Getting Acceptance Data

One customer was using a pricing model he had developed in Excel. We wrote tests that compared the output of our project's pricing code with the output from his Excel spreadsheet and then corrected our logic and formulas as necessary. This gave everyone confidence that critical business logic for pricing was correct and gave the customer the ability to easily modify acceptance criteria.

Using FIT, the customer defines a new feature with examples of its use. The customers, testers, and developers (based on the examples) then create tables that describe the possible input and output values for the code. The developer can then create test fixtures that compare the examples in the FIT tables with the output of the code being developed. The result of the tests—successes and failures—is displayed in an HTML page, making it easy for the users to see.

If your domain experts give you algorithms, calculations, or equations, provide them with a way of testing your implementation in isolation (see Practice 35, *Attack Problems in Isolation*, on page 139). Make those tests part of your test suite—you want to make sure you continue to provide the correct answers throughout the life of the project.

Create tests for core business logic. *Have your customers verify these tests in isolation, and exercise them automatically as part of your general test runs.*

What It Feels Like

It feels like cooperative unit testing: you're still writing the tests, but someone else is providing you the answers.

Keeping Your Balance

- Not all customers can give you correct data. If they had correct data already, they wouldn't need the new system.

- You may discover previously unknown bugs in the old system (be it computer or manual) or genuine issues that didn't exist before.

- Use the customer's business logic, but don't get bogged down documenting it extensively.

23 ▶ Measure Real Progress

"Please use your time sheets to report your progress. We'll use these for project planning. Always fill in 40 hours each week, regardless of how much you really worked."

The passage of time (which is usually way too fast) provides great feedback: what better way to determine whether you're on schedule than to see how long it's *actually* taking you, as opposed to what you had estimated?

Ah, but you say you're already tracking that, using time sheets. Unfortunately, in most corporations, time sheets are intended for payroll accounting and are not really meant to measure progress of work in software projects. If you worked sixty hours, for example, your boss probably asked you to fill in only forty hours in the time sheet—that's what accounting wants to see. Time sheets rarely represent the reality of work completed and therefore aren't useful for project planning, estimation, or measuring performance.

> Focus on where you're going

Even without time sheets, some developers have difficulties focusing on reality. Have you ever heard a developer report that he's 80% on a task? Day after day and week after week, still 80% done? That's not a useful measure at any rate; it's like being 80% **true** (unless you're a politician, **true** and **false** are boolean conditions). Instead of trying to calculate some bogus percentage of "doneness," try to determine how much work you have left. If you initially estimated the task to be 40 hours and after 35 hours you think there's another 30 hours of work, then that's the important measurement (honesty is important here; there's no sense in trying to hide the obvious).

When you do finally finish the task, keep track of how long it *really* took. Odds are, it probably took longer than you originally estimated. That's OK; just make a note of it for next time. For the next task you have to estimate, adjust your estimate based on this experience. If you underestimated a two-day task, and it took six, you were short by a factor of three. Unless there were unusual circumstances, maybe you should multiply your next estimate by three. You'll zig-zag around for awhile, under- and overestimating your effort, but over time, your

> ## Andy Says. . .
>
> ### Accounting for Time
>
> My sister-in-law once worked for a large, international consultancy. They had to account for their time in six-minute increments throughout the day, every day.
>
> They even had a code to track the time spent filling in the form to track your time. But instead of being 0, 9999, or some easy-to-remember code, it was the very convenient 948247401299-44b.
>
> This is why you don't want the accounting department's rules and constraints to leak out and spill over into the project.

estimates will converge, and you'll get a better sense of how long a given task will take.

It's also helpful to measure progress by keeping the road ahead very visible. The best way to do that is by using a *backlog*.

A backlog is just a list of tasks that still need to be completed. When a task is completed, it's removed from the backlog (logically; physically you might just cross it off or mark it as done to leave a list of accomplishments). As new tasks are introduced, they are prioritized and added to the backlog. You can have a personal backlog, a backlog for the current iteration, and a backlog for the project as a whole.[5]

With the backlog, you always know the next most important thing on which to work. As your estimation skill improves over time, you'll get a better and better idea of how long it might take as well.

It's a powerful technique to keep track of your real progress.

 Measure how much work is left. *Don't kid yourself—or your team—with irrelevant metrics. Measure the backlog of work to do.*

---

[5]For more details on using backlogs and The List as a personal and project management tool, see *Ship It!* [RG05].

Sprints in Scrum

In the Scrum method (Sch04), each iteration is known as a *sprint* and lasts 30 days. The sprint backlog holds tasks scheduled for the current iteration; it also shows the estimated number of hours left to complete each task.

On a daily basis, each team member updates the estimate of the number of hours they need to finish a task. At any point, if the total number of hours for all the tasks exceeds the number of hours left, then tasks have to be moved to the next iteration.

If there are more hours left in the month than estimated hours, then you can add tasks back in. Customers love it when you do that.

What It Feels Like

You feel comfortable that you know what has been done, what's left, and what your priorities are.

Keeping Your Balance

- Six-minute units are too fine-grained and aren't agile.

- Week-long or month-long units are too coarse-grained and aren't agile either.

- Focus on functionality, not the calendar.

- If you're spending so much time keeping track of how much time you're spending that you aren't spending enough time working on the project, then you're spending too much time keeping track of how much time you're spending. Get it?

- In a forty-hour work week, not all forty hours are available for you to write code for the project. Meetings, phone calls, email, and other related activities can take a substantial amount of time.

Listen to Users

"Users are always complaining. It's not your fault; they're just too stupid to read the stinkin' manual. It's not a bug; they just don't understand. They should know better."

Andy once worked for a large company that developed products for high-end Unix workstations. This wasn't the sort of environment where you could just run setup.exe or pkgadd to install the software. You had to copy files and tune various settings on your workstation.

Andy and his team thought everything was going well, until one day Andy was walking past the tech support area and overheard a support engineer laughing loudly into the phone: "Oh, it's not a bug; you made the same mistake *everyone* does." And it wasn't just this one engineer. The whole department was chuckling at the poor, naïve, stupid customers.

Apparently there was a situation where you, the hapless customer, had to go tweak some obscure system file to contain a magic value, or otherwise the application would not run at all. No error message, no crash, just a big black screen followed by an abrupt exit. Granted, a line in the installation instructions mentioned this fact, but apparently some 80% of the customers missed that fact and had to instead submit to abuse via the company's tech support line.

As we mention in Chapter 7, *Agile Debugging*, on page 131, you want to provide as much detail as possible when something goes wrong.

It's a bug

A black screen and inexplicable exit doesn't cut it. But worse, when this company received real feedback from its users, they laughed at their stupidity instead of addressing the problem.

Whether it's a bug in the product, a bug in the documentation, or a bug in our understanding of the user community, it's still the team's problem, not the user's.

Then there was the case of the expensive manufacturing shop-floor control system that none of the users would use. It seems the first step to using the system was to log on with their name and password, and the majority of the workers in this plant were illiterate. No one had ever bothered to ask them or get their feedback, so a completely useless system was installed. (The developers in question had to retool the entire GUI to be picture-based at huge expense.)

We go to great lengths to get feedback from code using unit tests and such, but it's all too easy to ignore the feedback from users. So not only do you need to talk to real users (not their managers or a surrogate such as a business analyst), you need to *listen* to them.

Even if they sound stupid.

 Every complaint holds a truth. *Find the truth, and fix the real problem.*

What It Feels Like

You don't get irate or dismissive of stupid complaints; you can look past that and see the real, underlying problem.

Keeping Your Balance

- There is no such thing as a stupid user.

- There *is* such a thing as a stupid, arrogant developer.

- "That's just the way it is" is not an answer.

- If the code can't be fixed, perhaps the documentation and training can be.

- Your users may have read all the documentation and will remember everything about your application all the time.

  But probably not.

*Any fool can make things bigger, more
complex, and more violent. It takes a touch
of genius—and a lot of courage—to move in
the opposite direction.*

▶ John Dryden,
    Epistle X—To Congreve

Chapter 6

Agile Coding

When you start on a new project from scratch, the code is easy to understand and work with. As you progress with your development, however, you may find the project slowly turns into a monster, eventually taking more developers and an inordinate amount of effort to keep it going.

What turns a project that started out so well into a project that becomes hard to handle? As you worked on the tasks, you probably were tempted to take some shortcuts to save time. Often, however, a shortcut helps you only postpone a problem instead of solving it (as we saw in Practice 2, *Quick Fixes Become Quicksand*, on page 16). It may come back to haunt you, and the rest of your team, as the schedule pressure mounts.

How can you keep the normal pressure in project development from creating stressful nightmares later? The easiest way is to keep your code well maintained. A small amount of effort each day while developing code can help you keep the code from rotting and keep the application from becoming hard to understand and maintain.

The practices in this chapter will help you develop code that's easier to understand, extend, and maintain for the duration of the project and beyond. These practices will give you a sanity check to prevent your code from turning into a monster.

To begin, it's better to be clear than clever as you *Program Intently and Expressively*, starting on page 103. Comments can be helpful or a dangerous distraction; you should always *Communicate in Code* (that's on page 108). Nothing in engineering comes for free; you have to decide what's more important and what the consequences of each decision are. You'll need to *Actively Evaluate Trade-Offs* (it's on page 113) to make the best decisions.

Just as the project develops in increments, you will want to *Code in Increments* as well. See how, starting on page 116. When writing code, it can be very hard to *Keep It Simple*—in fact, it's harder to write simple code than to write nasty, overly complicated code. But it's worth the effort, as we'll see on page 118.

Good object-oriented design principles suggest you should *Write Cohesive Code*, which we'll talk about on page 120. An excellent way to keep your code untangled and clean is to observe the *Tell, Don't Ask* principle, described on page 124. Finally, you can keep your code flexible in an uncertain future by designing the system such that you can *Substitute by Contract*, which we'll look at on page 127.

Program Intently and Expressively

"Code that works and is understandable is nice, but it's more important to be clever. You're paid for being smart; show us how good you are."

Hoare on Software Design
by C.A.R. Hoare

There are two ways of creating a software design. One way is to make it so simple that there are obviously no deficiencies. And the other way is to make it so complicated that there are no obvious deficiencies.

You've probably seen a lot of code that's hard to understand, that's hard to maintain, and (worst of all) has errors. You can tell code is bad when developers circle around it like spectators near a UFO—with the same mix of apprehension, confusion, and helplessness. What good is a piece of code if no one can understand how it works?

When developing code, you should always choose readability over convenience. Code will be read many, many more times than it is written; it's well worth it to take a small performance hit during writing if it makes the reading easier. In fact, code clarity comes before execution performances as well.

For instance, if default or optional arguments are going to make your code less readable, less understandable, or buggier, it would be better to specify the arguments explicitly, rather than cause later confusion.

When you modify a piece of code to fix a bug or add new feature, try to approach it systematically. First, you have to understand what the code does and how it works. Then, you need to figure out what you're going to change. You then make your changes and test. The first of these steps, understanding the code, is often the hardest. If someone hands you code that's easy to understand, they're making your life a lot easier. Honoring the Golden Rule, you owe it to them to make your own code easy to read.

One way to make code understandable is to make it obvious to see what's happening. Let's look at some examples:

```
coffeeShop.PlaceOrder(2);
```

Reading the above code, you can probably figure out that we're placing an order at a coffee shop. But, what in the world is 2? Does that mean two cups of coffee? Two shots? Or is it the size of the cup? The only way for you to be certain is to look at the method definition or the documentation. This code isn't easy to understand by reading.

So we add some comments to make the code easier to understand:

```
coffeeShop.PlaceOrder(2 /* large cup */);
```

That's a tad better, but this is an occasion where commenting is used to compensate for poor code (Practice 26, *Communicate in Code*, on page 108).

Java 5 and .NET (among others) have the concept of enumerated values. Let's use it. We can define an enum named CoffeeCupSize in C# as the following:

```
public enum CoffeeCupSize
{
    Small,
    Medium,
    Large
}
```

Then we can use it to order coffee:

```
coffeeShop.PlaceOrder(CoffeeCupSize.Large);
```

This code makes it obvious that we are placing an order for a large[1] cup of coffee.

As a developer, you should always be asking yourself whether there are ways to make your code easier to understand. Here's another one:

```
Line 1  public int compute(int val)
        {
            int result = val << 1;
            //... more code ...
5           return result;
        }
```

What's up with the shift operator in line 3? If you're an experienced bit twiddler or familiar with logic design or assembly programming, then you may have figured that we just multiplied the value in *val* by 2.

---

[1]That's *venti* to you Starbucks fans.

> ### The PIE Principle
>
> Code you write must clearly communicate your intent and must be expressive. By doing so, your code will be readable and understandable. Since your code is not confusing, you will also avoid some potential errors. Program Intently and Expressively.

But what about folks who may not have that background—will they figure that out? Perhaps you have some inexperienced team members who only recently made a career change into programming. These folks will scratch their heads until their hair falls out.[2] Although the code may be efficient, it lacks intent and expressiveness.

Shifting to multiply is an example of unnecessary and dangerous performance optimization. result = val*2 is clearer, works, and is probably even more efficient given a decent compiler (old habits die hard; see Practice 7, *Know When to Unlearn*, on page 35). Instead of being too clever and opaque, follow the PIE principle: Program Intently and Expressively (see the sidebar on this page).

Violating the PIE principle can go beyond readability or understandability of code—it can affect its correctness. Here's a C# method that tries to synchronize calls to the MakeCoffee() method of a CoffeeMaker:

```
public void MakeCoffee()
{
  lock(this)
  {
    // ... operation
  }
}
```

The author of this method wanted to define a critical section—at most one thread may execute the code in *operation* at any instant. To do that, the writer claimed a lock on the CoffeeMaker instance. A thread may execute this method only if it can acquire that lock. (In Java, you would use **synchronized** instead of **lock**, but the idea is the same.)

Although the code may look reasonable to any Java or .NET programmer, it has two subtle problems. First, the lock is too sweeping, and

---

[2]Yeah, that's not a bald spot; it's a solar panel for a coding machine....

second, you are claiming a lock on a globally visible object. Let's look at both these issues further.

Assume the coffeemaker can also dispense hot water, for those fans of a little Earl Gray in the morning. Suppose I want to synchronize the GetWater() method, so I call lock(this) within it. This synchronizes any code that uses **lock** on the CoffeeMaker instance. That means you cannot make coffee and get hot water at the same time. Is that my intent, or did the lock become too sweeping? It's not clear from reading the code, and you, the user of this code, are left wondering.

Also, the MakeCoffee() method implementation claims a lock on the CoffeeMaker object, which is visible to the rest of the application. What if instead you lock the CoffeeMaker instance in one thread and then call the MakeCoffee() method on that instance from another thread? At best it may lead to poor performance, and at worst it may lead to deadlock.

Let's apply the PIE principle to this code, modifying it to make it more explicit. You want to keep more than one thread from executing the MakeCoffee() method at the same time. So, why not create an object specifically for that purpose and lock it?

```
private object makeCoffeeLock = new object();

public void MakeCoffee()
{
  lock(makeCoffeeLock)
  {
    // ... operation
  }
}
```

This code addresses both the concerns we discussed—we rely on an explicit object to synchronize, and we express our intent more clearly.

When writing code, use language features to be expressive. Use method names that convey the intent; name method parameters to help readers understand their purpose. Exceptions convey what could go wrong and how to program defensively; use them and name them appropriately. Good coding discipline can help make the code more understandable while reducing the need for unnecessary comments and other documentation.

Write code to be clear, not clever. *Express your intentions clearly to the reader of the code. Unreadable code isn't clever.*

What It Feels Like

You feel you—or anyone else on the team—can understand a piece of code you wrote a year ago and know exactly what it does in just one reading.

Keeping Your Balance

- What's obvious to you now may not be obvious to others, or to you in a year's time. Consider your coding to be a kind of time capsule that will be opened in some unknowing future.

- There is no later. If you can't do it right now, you won't be able to do it right later.

- Writing with intent doesn't mean creating more classes or types. It's not an excuse for overabstraction.

- Use coupling that matches the situation: for instance, loose coupling via a hash table is intended for a situation where the components really are loosely coupled in real life. Don't use it for components that are tightly coupled, because that doesn't express your intent clearly.

Communicate in Code

"Comments should help out when the code is too tangled to read. Explain exactly what the code is doing, line by line. Don't worry about why; just tell us what on Earth it's doing."

Programmers generally hate writing documentation. That's because most documentation is kept separate from the code and becomes hard to keep up-to-date. Besides violating the DRY principle (Don't Repeat Yourself, in [HT00]), it can lead to misleading documentation, which is generally worse than none at all.

You need to document your code in two ways: using the code itself and using comments to communicate noncode issues.

If you have to read through a method in order to understand what it does, you wind up investing a lot of time and effort before you can use that method in your own code. On the other hand, a few lines of comments that describe the behavior of the method can make your life easier. You quickly learn its intent, what its expectations are, and what you need to watch out for—saving you a lot of effort.

Don't comment to cover up

Should you document all your code? To some extent, yes. But that doesn't mean you need comments for most of the code you write, especially within the body of your methods. Source code should be understandable not because it has comments but because of its elegance and clarity—proper use of variable names, good use of whitespace, good separation of logic, and concise expression.

Naming is a big deal. The names of program elements are often all the reader of the code has to go on.[3] By using well-chosen names, you can convey a lot of intent and information to the reader. On the other hand, using artificial naming schemes (such as the now-rebarbative Hungarian Notation) can make the code harder to read and understand. These schemes bombard you with low-level data typing infor-

---

[3]In *The Wizard of Earthsea* books, for example, knowing the true name of something gives one complete power over it. Magical control via naming is a fairly common theme in literature and mythology and has a similar effect in software.

mation hard-coded in the names of variables and methods and make for brittle, inflexible code.

With well-chosen names and clear execution paths, code needs very few comments. In fact, when Andy and coauthor Dave Thomas wrote the first book on the Ruby programming language [TH01], they were able to document virtually the entire language just by reading the code to the Ruby interpreter. And it was a good thing that the code spoke for itself, instead of relying on comments: Ruby's creator, Yukihiro Matsumoto, is Japanese, and neither Andy nor Dave speak any Japanese beyond "sukiyaki" and "sake."

What makes a good name? A good name is one that conveys a lot of correct information to the reader. A bad name conveys nothing, and a terrible name conveys *incorrect* information.

For instance, a method named readAccount() that actually writes address information to the disk would count as terrible (and yes, that really happened. See [HT00]).

foo is a great and historically significant temporary variable name, but it conveys *no* information as to the author's intent. Fight the urge to use cryptic variable names. Cryptic doesn't necessarily mean short: i is traditionally used as a loop index variable in many languages, and s is generally used for a String of some sort. That's idiomatic in many languages and, even though short, isn't necessarily cryptic. Using s for a loop index variable in those environments would be a really bad idea, and using indexvar isn't really any better. You don't need to belabor the obvious with verbose variable names.

You'll encounter the same issues with comments that convey the obvious, such as //Constructor next to a class constructor. Unfortunately, this kind of comment is very prevalent—usually inserted by overly helpful IDEs. At best, all it does it add noise to the source code. At worst, it can end up being incorrect over the course of time.

Many comments just don't convey anything useful. For instance, what help do you get from the comment "This method allows you to passthrough" for the passthrough() method? This kind of comment is distracting and can easily get out of sync (as when you finally rename the method to be sendToHost()).

It can be helpful to use comments to set up a road map of sorts to point readers in the right direction. For each class or module in your code, you can add a short description of its purpose and any special requirements it has. For each method in the class, you might want to mention some of the following:

- Purpose: Why does this method exist?

- Requirements (pre-conditions): What inputs do we need, and what state must the object be in, for this method to work?

- Promises (post-conditions): What state is the object in, and what values are returned, on successful completion of this method?

- Exceptions: What can go wrong, and what exceptions may be thrown?

Thanks to tools such as RDoc, javadoc, and ndoc, it's easy to create useful, well-formatted documentation directly from comments embedded in your code. These tools take your comments and produce pretty, hyperlinked HTML output.

Here are excerpts from a piece of documented code in C#. Normal comments are represented by //, and comments intended for documentation use /// (which is still a legal comment, of course).

```
using System;
namespace Bank
{
    /// <summary>
    /// A BankAccount represents a customer's non-secured deposit
    /// account in the domain (see Reg 47.5, section 3).
    /// </summary>
    public class BankAccount
    {
        ...
        /// <summary>
        /// Increases balance by the given amount.
        /// Requirements: can only deposit a positive amount.
        /// </summary>
        ///
        /// <param name="depositAmount">The amount to deposit, already
        /// validated and converted to a Money object
        /// </param>
        ///
        /// <param name="depositSource">Origination of the monies
        /// (see  FundSource for details)
        /// </param>
        ///
        /// <returns>Resulting balance as a convenience
        /// </returns>
```

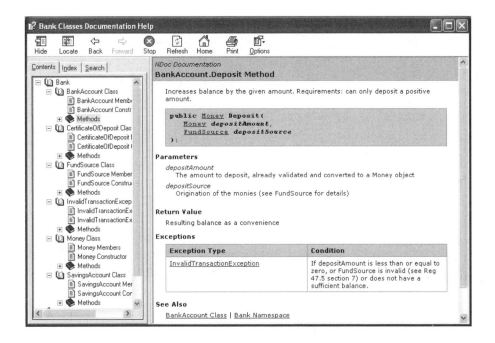

Figure 6.1: DOCUMENTATION EXTRACTED FROM CODE USING NDOC

```
    ///
    /// <exception cref="InvalidTransactionException">
    /// If depositAmount is less than or equal to zero, or FundSource
    /// is invalid (see Reg 47.5 section 7)
    /// or does not have a sufficient balance.
    /// </exception>

    public Money Deposit(Money depositAmount, FundSource depositSource)
    {
        ...
    }
  }
}
```

Figure 6.1 shows the documentation created using ndoc from the comments in the C# code example. Javadoc for Java, RDoc for Ruby, and others work pretty much the same way.

This sort of documentation is not just for people outside your team, or organization. Imagine you are asked to fix some code a few months after you wrote it: your life would be a lot easier if you could just quickly look at the comments at the top of the method and glean from them the important details you need to know. After all, if a method will work only when there's a full solar eclipse, it would be nice to know that up-front, without having to examine the code in detail—or waiting another ten years or so.

Code will always be read many more times than written, so the little extra effort that is required to document your code when writing it will pay you back handsomely in the end.

 Comment to communicate. *Document code using well-chosen, meaningful names. Use comments to describe its purpose and constraints. Don't use commenting as a substitute for good code.*

What It Feels Like

Comments feel like helpful friends; you can read them and quickly scan code to fully understand what it's doing and why.

Keeping Your Balance

- Blaise Pascal famously said he didn't have time to write a short letter, so he had to write a long one. Take the time to write a short comment.

- Don't use comments in places where real code can convey the intent instead.

- Commenting what the code does isn't that useful; instead, comment why it does it.

- When you override methods, preserve the intent and the comments that describe the purpose and constraints of the original method.

Actively Evaluate Trade-Offs

"Performance, productivity, elegance, cost, and time to market are the most important, critical issues in software development. You have to maximize all of them."

You may be part of a team where the manager or customer places a lot of emphasis on the appearance of your application. There are also teams where clients place much importance on performance. Within the team, you may find a lead developer or architect who emphasizes following the "right" paradigm more than anything else. Such exclusive emphasis—on anything—without regard to whether it's essential for the success of the project is a recipe for disaster.

It is reasonable to think that performance is important, because poor performance can kill an application's chance of success in the market. However, if your application's performance is reasonable, should you still work on getting it faster? Probably not. Many other aspects of an application are also important. Rather than spend time eking out the last millisecond, perhaps it's more important to bring the application to market sooner, with less development effort and at a lower cost.

For example, consider the case of a .NET Windows application that has to communicate with a remote Windows server. You can choose between using .NET remoting and web services to implement this facility. Now, the very mention of web services provokes some developers to say, "We're going from Windows to Windows, and the literature recommends .NET remoting in this case. Besides, web services are slow, and we'll have performance problems." That is, indeed, the party line.

However, in this case, going the web services route was easier to develop. A quick measure of performance showed that the size of the XML[4] was pretty small, and the time spent in creating and parsing XML was negligible compared to the time the application itself took to respond. Going the web services route not only saved time in the short run but proved to be wiser when the team was forced to switch to using a third-party service later.

---

[4]XML documents are much like humans—they are cute and fun to deal with when they're small but can get really annoying as they grow bigger.

> ## Andy Says...
>
> ### Taking Things to Extremes
>
> I once had a client who was a firm believer in configurability, so much so, in fact, that their application had something like 10,000 configuration variables. Adding code became tortuous because of the overhead of maintaining the configuration application and database. But they swore they needed this level of flexibility because every one of their customers had different requirements, and needed different settings.
>
> But they had only nineteen customers and didn't expect to grow beyond fifty. That was not a good trade-off.

Consider an application where you have to fetch data from a database and tabularize it for display. You could use an elegant object-oriented approach to get the data from the database, creating objects and returning them to the UI tier. In the UI tier, you can then fetch the data from the objects and populate your table. Other than being elegant, what are the benefits of this approach?

Maybe you could simply ask the data tier to return a dataset or collection of data and then populate the table with that data. You could avoid the overhead of object creation and destruction. If all you need is to display data, why go through the hassle of creating objects? By not doing OO by the book, you will have saved effort (and gained some performance as well). There are significant drawbacks to this approach, of course, but the point is to be *aware* of them, not just take the long road out of habit.

After all, the cost of development and time you take to get to market both have significant impact on the success of your application. And because computers are getting cheaper and faster every day, you can spend money on hardware to buy performance and invest the time that you save on other aspects of the application.

Of course, that is true only to a point: if your hardware needs are so great that you require a large grid of computers and a sizeable support staff to keep it running (something the size of Google, say), then the balance may tip back the other way.

But who decides whether the performance is adequate or whether the look of the application is "dazzling" enough? The customers or stakeholders must evaluate and make this decision (see Practice 10, *Let Customers Make Decisions*, on page 47). If your team thinks the performance can be improved or you can make something more attractive, then consult the stakeholder and let them decide where you should focus your efforts.

No one best solution fits all circumstances. You have to evaluate the problem on hand and arrive at a solution that is the most suitable. **No best solution** Each design is very specific to the particular problem—the better ones are found by explicitly evaluating the trade-offs.

Actively evaluate trade-offs. *Consider performance, convenience, productivity, cost, and time to market. If performance is adequate, then focus on improving the other factors. Don't complicate the design for the sake of perceived performance or elegance.*

What It Feels Like

Even though you can't have everything, it should feel like you have the important things—the features important to the customer.

Keeping Your Balance

- If you're investing extra effort now for a perceived benefit later, make sure the investment will pay off (most of the time, it probably won't).

- True high-performance systems are designed that way from the beginning.

- Premature optimization is the root of all evil.[5]

- A solution or approach you have used in the past may—*or may not*—be appropriate to the current problem. Don't automatically assume either position; check it out.

---

[5]Donald Knuth's pithy summary of Hoare's dictum[Knu92]

28 ▶ Code in Increments

"Real programmers work for hours and hours straight, without a break, without even looking up. Don't break your flow to stop and compile: just keep typing!"

When you're driving on a long trip, does it make sense to hold the wheel firmly in one position, stare straight ahead, and then just floor the gas for a couple of hours? Of course not. You have to steer. You have to be constantly aware of traffic. You have to check your gas gauge. You have to stop for fuel, food, and other necessities, and so on.[6]

Don't code for hours, or even minutes, without stopping to make sure you're on the right path—by testing what you produce. Instead, code in short *increments*. You'll find that coding in increments helps you refine and structure the code as you go along. The code is less likely to become complicated or messy; you build the code based on the on-going feedback from writing and testing in increments.

When you write and test incrementally, you tend to create methods that are smaller and classes that are more cohesive. You are not heads-down, blindly writing large pieces of code in one shot. Instead, you are constantly evaluating how the code is shaping up, making many small adjustments rather than a few really, really large ones.

While you are writing code, constantly look for small ways to improve it. You might work on its readability. Perhaps you discover that you can break a method into smaller methods, thus making it more testable. Many of the small improvements you make fall under the general heading of *Refactoring* (discussed in Martin Fowler's *Refactoring: Improving the Design of Existing Code* [FBB+99]). You can use test-first development (see Practice 20, *Use It Before You Build It*, on page 85) as a way of enforcing incremental development. The key is to keep doing something small and useful, rather than saving up for a single long session of coding or refactoring.

That's the agile approach.

---

[6]Kent Beck introduced the driving analogy—and the importance of steering—in *XP Explained* [Bec00].

Write code in short edit/build/test cycles. *It's better than coding for an extended period of time. You'll create code that's clearer, simpler, and easier to maintain.*

What It Feels Like

You feel the urge to run a build/test cycle after writing a few lines of code. You don't want to go too far without getting feedback.

Keeping Your Balance

- If the build and test cycle takes too long, you won't want to do it often enough. Make sure the tests run quickly.

- Pausing to think and "zoom out" from the code details while the compile and test is running is a good way to stay on track.

- When you take a break, take a real break. Step away from the keyboard.

- Refactor tests as well as code and as frequently.

▶ 29 Keep It Simple

"Software is complex business. Any fool can write simple, elegant software. You'll get fame and recognition (not to mention job security) by writing the most sophisticated, complex programs possible."

Perhaps you come across an article that describes a design idea, expressing it as a pattern with a fancy name. When you put the magazine down, the chances are that the code in front of you suddenly looks as if it would benefit from the new idea—that pattern—you picked up. Ask yourself whether you really need that and how it will help with the specific problem on hand. Ask yourself whether specific problems forced you to use that solution. Don't succumb to the pressure to overdesign and overcomplicate your code.

Andy once knew a fellow who was so fascinated by design patterns, he wanted to use all of them. At once. On one small, several-hundred-line piece of code. He managed to get about seventeen of the original GOF book [GHJV95] patterns involved in the hapless program before he was discovered.

That's not how you write agile code.

The problem is that many developers tend to confuse effort with complexity. If you look at any given solution and say that it is simple and easy to understand, chances are you'll make its designer unhappy. Many developers take pride in creating complexity: they often beam with pride if you say, "Wow, that is hard—it should've taken a lot of effort to arrive at!" On the contrary, you should be proud of creating a simple design that works well.

Simple is not simplistic

Simplicity is widely misunderstood (in programming as well as life in general). It doesn't mean simplistic, amateurish, or insufficient in any way. Quite the opposite. Simplicity is often much more difficult to achieve than an overly complex, kludgey solution.

Simplicity, in coding or writing, is like a chef's fine reduction sauce. You start with a lot of wine, stock, and spices and you carefully boil it down to a super-concentrated essence. That's what good code should taste like—not a large watery mess but a rich, fine sauce.

> ## Andy Says...
>
> ### What Is elegance?
>
> Elegant code is immediately obvious in its utility and clarity. But the solution isn't something you would have thought of easily. That is, elegance is easy to understand and recognize but much harder to create.

One of the best ways to measure the quality of design is to listen to your intuition. Intuition isn't magic: it's the culmination of your experience and skill. When you look at a design, listen to that voice in your head. If something bothers you, then it's time to get an understanding of what's wrong. A good design makes you feel comfortable.

Develop the simplest solution that works. *Incorporate patterns, principles, and technology only if you have a compelling reason to use them.*

What It Feels Like

It feels right when there isn't any line of code you could remove and still deliver all the needed features. Code is easy to follow and correct.

Keeping Your Balance

- Code can almost always be refined even further, but at a certain point you won't be getting any real benefit from continued improvements. Stop and move on before you hit that point.

- Keep the goal in mind: simple, readable code. Trying to force elegance is similar to premature optimization and just as damaging.

- Simple solutions must, of course, be adequate—compromising features for simplicity is merely *simplistic*.

- Terse is not simple; it's merely uncommunicative.

- One person's simplicity may be another person's complexity.

30 ▶ Write Cohesive Code

"You are about to write some new code, and the first decision you need to make is where to put it. It doesn't really matter where it goes, so just go ahead and add it to the class that happens to be open in your IDE now. It's easier to keep track of code when it's all in one big class or component anyway."

Cohesion is a measure of how functionally related the members of a component (package, module, or assembly) are. A higher value of cohesion indicates that the members work toward one feature or set of features. A lower value of cohesion indicates that the members provide a disparate set of features.

Imagine tossing all your clothes into one drawer. When you need to find a pair of socks, you will have to wade through all the clothes you have in there—your pants, underwear, T-shirts, etc.—before you can find the pair of socks you want. It can be very frustrating, especially when you are in a hurry. Now, imagine keeping all your socks in one drawer (in matching pairs), all your T-shirts in another, and so on. The effort to find a pair of socks is merely to open the right drawer.

Similarly, how you organize a component can make a big difference in your productivity and overall code maintenance. When you decide to create a class, ask yourself whether the functionality provided by this class is similar to and closely related to the functionality of other classes already in that component. This is cohesion at the component level.

Classes are also subject to cohesion. A class is cohesive if its methods and properties work together to implement one feature (or a closely related set of functionality).

Consider Mr. Charles Hess's 1866 patent of a "Convertible Piano, Couch, and Bureau" (Figure 6.2, on the facing page). According to his patent claim, it features the "...addition of couch, bureau...to fill up the unused space underneath the piano...." He goes on to justify the need for his convertible piano. You may have seen your share of classes that resemble this invention in your projects. There isn't much cohesion here, and one can imagine that the maintenance on this beast (changing the sheets, tuning the piano, etc.) is probably pretty difficult.

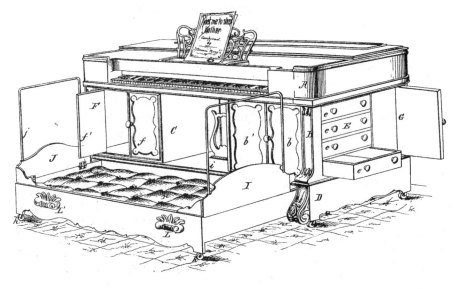

Figure 6.2: U.S. PATENT 56,413: CONVERTIBLE PIANO, COUCH, AND BUREAU

For an example from this century, Venkat came across a twenty-page web application written using ASP. Each page started out with HTML and contained a serious amount of VBScript with embedded SQL statements to access a database. The client was rightfully concerned that this application had gotten out of hand and was hard to maintain. If each page contains presentation logic, business logic, and code for data access, too much is going on in one place.

Suppose you decide to make a slight change to the database table schema. This small change will result in a change to all the pages in this application and also multiple changes in each page—this application becomes a disaster quickly.

If instead the application had used a middle-tier object (such as a COM component) to access the database, the impact of change in the database schema would have been localized, making the code easier to maintain.

The consequences of having low cohesion are pretty severe. Suppose you have a class that implements five disparate features. This class will have to change if the requirements or details of any of these five features change. If a class (or a component) changes too frequently, such a change may ripple through the system and will result in higher maintenance and cost. Consider another class that implements just one feature. This second class will change less frequently. Similarly, a component that is more cohesive has fewer reasons to be modified and is thus more stable. According to the Single Responsibility Principle (see *Agile Software Development: Principles, Patterns, and Practices* [Mar02]), a module should have only one reason to change.

A number of design techniques can help. For instance, we often use the Model-View-Controller (MVC) pattern to separate the presentation logic, the control, and the model. This pattern is effective because it allows you to achieve higher cohesion—the classes in the model contain one kind of functionality, those in the control contain another kind, and those in the view are solely concerned with UI.

Cohesion affects reusability of a component as well. The granularity of a component is an important design consideration. According to the Reuse Release Equivalency principle ([Mar02]), "Granularity of reuse is the same as the granularity of release." That is, a user of your library should have a need for the entire library and not only a part of it. Fail to follow this principle, and users of your component are forced to use only part of the component you have released. Unfortunately, they'll still be affected by updates to the parts they don't care about. The bigger the package, the less reusable it is.

Keep classes focused and components small. *Avoid the temptation to build large classes or components or miscellaneous catchall classes.*

What It Feels Like

Classes and components feel tightly focused: each does one thing, and does it well. Bugs are easy to track down, and code is easy to modify because responsibilities are clear.

Keeping Your Balance

- It's possible to break something down into so many little parts that it isn't useful anymore. A box of cotton fibers isn't helpful when you need a sock.[7]

- Cohesive code can be changed proportionally to the change in requirements. Consider how many code changes you need to implement a simple functional change.[8]

---

[7]You might call this a "Spaghetti OOs" system.

[8]One reviewer told us of a system that needed sixteen team members and six managers to add one field to a form. That's a pretty clear warning sign of a noncohesive system.

Tell, Don't Ask

"Don't trust other objects. After all, they were written by other people, or even by you last month when you weren't as smart. Get the information you need from others, and then do your own calculations and make your own decisions. Don't give up control to others!"

"Procedural code gets information and then makes decisions. Object-oriented code tells objects to do things." Alec Sharp [Sha97] hit the nail on the head with that observation. But it's not limited to the object-oriented paradigm; any agile code should follow this same path.

As the caller, you should *not* make decisions based on the state of the called object and then change the state of that object. The logic you are implementing should be the called object's responsibility, not yours. For you to make decisions outside the object violates its encapsulation and provides a fertile breeding ground for bugs.

David Bock illustrates this well with the tale of the paperboy and the wallet.[9] Suppose the paperboy comes to your door, requesting his payment for the week. You turn around and let the paperboy pull your wallet out of your back pocket, take the two bucks (you hope), and put the wallet back. The paper boy then drives off in his shiny new Jaguar.

The paperboy, as the "caller" in this transaction, should simply tell the customer to pay $2. There's no inquiry into the customer's financial state, or the condition of the wallet, and no decision on the paperboy's part. All of that is the customer's responsibility, not the paperboy's. Agile code should work the same way.

Keep commands separate from queries

A helpful side technique related to *Tell, Don't Ask* is known as *command-query separation* [Mey97]. The idea is to categorize each of your functions and methods as either a command or a query and document them as such in the source code (it helps if all the commands are grouped together and all the queries are grouped together).

A routine acting as a command will likely change the state of the object and might also return some useful value as a convenience. A query just

---

[9]http://www.javaguy.org/papers/demeter.pdf

> **Beware of Side Effects**
>
> Have you ever heard someone say, "Oh—we're just calling that method because of its side effects." That's pretty much on par with defending an odd bit of architecture by saying, "Well, it's like that because it used to...."
>
> Statements such as these are clear warning signs of a fragile, not agile, design.
>
> Relying on side effects or living with an increasingly twisted design that just doesn't match reality are urgent indications you need to redesign and refactor the code.

gives you information about the state of the object and does not modify the externally visible state of the object.

That is, queries should be side effect free as seen from the outside world (you may want to do some pre-calculation or caching behind the scenes as needed, but fetching the value of X in the object should not change the value of Y).

Mentally framing methods as *commands* helps reinforce the idea of *Tell, Don't Ask*. Additionally, keeping queries as side effect free is just good practice anyway, because you can use them freely in unit tests, call them from assertions, or from the debugger, all without changing the state of the application.

Explicitly considering queries separately from commands also gives you the opportunity to ask yourself *why* you're exposing a particular piece of data. Do you really need to do so? What would a caller do with it? Perhaps there should be a related command instead.

Tell, don't ask. *Don't take on another object's or component's job. Tell it what to do, and stick to your own job.*

What It Feels Like

Smalltalk uses the concept of "message passing" instead of method calls. *Tell, Don't Ask* feels like you're sending messages, not calling functions.

Keeping Your Balance

- Objects that are just giant data holders are suspect. Sometimes you need such things, but maybe not as often as you think.

- It's OK for a command to return data as a convenience (it'd be nice to be able to retrieve that data separately, too, if that's needed).

- It's not OK for an innocent-looking query to change the state of an object.

32 ▶ Substitute by Contract

*"Deep inheritance hierarchies are great. If you need functional-
ity from some other class, just inherit from it! And don't worry
if your new class breaks things; your callers can just change
their code. It's their problem, not yours."*

A key way to keep systems flexible is by letting new code take the place
of existing code without the existing code knowing the difference. For
instance, you might need to add a new type of encryption to a communications infrastructure or implement a better search algorithm using
the same interface. As long as the interface remains the same, you are
free to change the implementation without changing any other code.
That's easier said than done, however, so we need a little bit of guidance to do it correctly. For that, we'll turn to Barbara Liskov.

Liskov's Substitution principle [Lis88] tells us that "Any derived class
object must be substitutable wherever a base class object is used, without the need for the user to know the difference." In other words, code
that uses methods in base classes must be able to use objects of derived
classes without modification.

What does that mean exactly? Suppose you have a simple method in
a class that sorts a list of strings and returns a new list. You might
invoke it like this:

```
utils = new BasicUtils();
...
sortedList = utils.sort(aList);
```

Now suppose you subclass the BasicUtils class and make a new sort()
method that uses a much better, faster sort algorithm:

```
utils = new FasterUtils();
...
sortedList = utils.sort(aList);
```

Note the call to sort() is the same; a FasterUtils object is perfectly substitutable for a BasicUtils object. The code that calls utils.sort() could be
handed a utils of either type, and it would work fine.

But if you made a subclass of BasicUtils that changed the meaning of
sort—returning a list that sorted in reverse order, perhaps—then you've
grossly violated the Substitution principle.

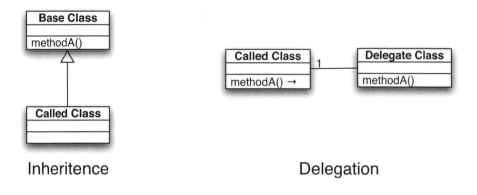

Inheritence   Delegation

Figure 6.3: DELEGATION VERSUS INHERITANCE

To comply with the Substitution principle, your derived class services (methods) should *require no more, and promise no less,* than the corresponding methods of the base class; it needs to be freely substitutable. This is an important consideration when designing class inheritance hierarchies.

Inheritance is one of the most abused concepts in OO modeling and programming. If you violate the Substitution principle, your inheritance hierarchy may still provide code reusability but will not help with extensibility. The user of your class hierarchy may now have to examine the type of the object it is given in order to know how to handle it. As new classes are introduced, that code has to constantly be reevaluated and revised. That's not an agile approach.

But help is available. Your compiler may help you enforce the LSP, at least to some extent. For example, consider method access modifiers. In Java, the overriding method's access modifier must be the same or more lenient than the modifier of the overridden method. That is, if the base method is protected, the derived overriding method must be protected or public. In C# and VB .NET, the access protection of the overridden method and the overriding method are required to be the same.

Consider a class Base with a method findLargest() that throws an IndexOutOfRangeException. Based on the documentation, a user of this class will prepare to catch that exception if thrown. Now, assume you inherit the class Derived from Base, override the method findLargest(), and in the new method throw a different exception. Now, if an instance of Derived is used by code expecting an object of class Base, that code may receive an unexpected exception. Your Derived class is not substitutable wherever Base is used. Java avoids this problem by not allowing you to throw any new kind of checked exceptions from the overriding methods, unless the exception itself derives from one of the exception classes thrown from the overridden method (of course, for unchecked exceptions such as RuntimeException, the compiler won't help you).

Unfortunately, Java violates the Substitution principle as well. The java.util.Stack class derives from the java.util.Vector class. If you (inadvertently) send an object of Stack to a method that expects an instance of Vector, the elements in the Stack can be inserted or removed in an order inconsistent with its intended behavior.

When using inheritance, ask yourself whether your derived class is substitutable in place of the base class. If the answer is no, then ask yourself why you are using inheritance. If the answer is to reuse code in the base class when developing your new class, then you should

Use inheritance for *is-a*; use delegation for *has-a* or *uses-a*

probably use composition instead. *Composition* is where an object of your class contains and uses an object of another class, delegating responsibilities to the contained object (this technique is also known as *delegation*).

Figure 6.3, on the preceding page shows the difference. Here, a caller invoking methodA() in Called Class will get it automatically from Base Class via inheritance. In the delegation model, the Called Class has to explicitly forward the method call to the contained delegate.

When should you use inheritance versus delegation?

- If your new class can be used in place of the existing class and the relationship between them can be described as *is-a*, then use inheritance.

- If your new class needs to simply use the existing class and the relationship can be described as *has-a* or *uses-a*, then use delegation.

You may argue that in the case of delegation you have to write lots of tiny methods that route method calls to the contained object. In inheritance, you don't need these, because the public methods of the base class are readily available in the derived class. By itself, that's not a good enough reason to use inheritance.

You can write a good script or a nice IDE macro to help you write these few lines of code or use a better language/environment that supports a more automatic form of delegation (Ruby does this nicely, for instance).

 Extend systems by substituting code. *Add and enhance features by substituting classes that honor the interface contract. Delegation is almost always preferable to inheritance.*

What It Feels Like

It feels sneaky; you can sneak a replacement component into the code base without any of the rest of the code knowing about it to achieve new and improved functionality.

Keeping Your Balance

- Delegation is usually more flexible and adaptable than inheritance.

- Inheritance isn't evil, just misunderstood.

- If you aren't sure what an interface really promises or requires, it will be hard to provide an implementation that honors it.

You might get the impression that experienced woodworkers never make mistakes. I can assure you that isn't true. Pros simply know how to salvage their goofs.

► Jeff Miller, furniture maker and author

Chapter 7

Agile Debugging

Even on the most talented agile projects, things will go wrong. Bugs, errors, defects, mistakes—whatever you want to call them, they will happen.

The real problem with debugging is that it is not amenable to a time box. You can time box a design meeting and decide to go with the best idea at the end of some fixed time. But with a debugging session, an hour, a day, or a week may come and go and find you no closer to finding and fixing the problem.

You really can't afford that sort of open-ended exposure on a project. So, we have some techniques that might help, from keeping track of previous solutions to providing more helpful clues in the event of a problem.

To reuse your knowledge and effort better, it can help to *Keep a Solutions Log*, and we'll see how on the following page. When the compiler warns you that something is amiss, you need to assume that *Warnings Are Really Errors* and address them right away (that's on page 135).

It can be very hard—even impossible—to track down problems in the middle of an entire system. You have a much better chance at finding the problem when you *Attack Problems in Isolation*, as we'll see on page 139. When something does go wrong, don't hide the truth. Unlike some government cover-up, you'll want to *Report All Exceptions*, as described on page 142. Finally, when you do report that something has gone awry, you have to be considerate of users, and *Provide Useful Error Messages*. We'll see why on page 144.

Keep a Solutions Log

"Do you often get that déjà vu feeling during development? Do you often get that déjà vu feeling during development? That's OK. You figured it out once. You can figure it out again."

Facing problems (and solving them) is a way of life for developers. When a problem arises, you want to solve it quickly. If a similar problem occurs again, you want to remember what you did the first time and fix it more quickly the next time. Unfortunately, sometimes you'll see a problem that looks the same as something you've seen before but can't remember the fix. This happens to us all the time.

Can't you just search the Web for an answer? After all, the Internet has grown to be this incredible resource, and you might as well put that to good use. Certainly searching the Web for an answer is better than wasting time in isolated efforts. However, it can be *very* time-consuming. Sometimes you find the answers you're looking for; other times, you end up reading a lot of opinions and ideas instead of real solutions. It might be comforting to see how many other developers have had the same problem, but what you need is a solution.

Don't get burned twice

To be more productive than that, maintain a log of problems faced and solutions found. When a problem appears, instead of saying, "Man, I've seen this before, but I have no clue how I fixed it," you can quickly look up the solution you've used in the past. Engineers have done this for years: they call them *daylogs*.

You can choose any format that suits your needs. Here are some items that you might want to include in your entries:

- Date of the problem
- Short description of the problem or issue
- Detailed description of the solution
- References to articles, and URLs, that have more details or related information
- Any code segments, settings, and snapshots of dialogs that may be part of the solution or help you further understand the details

> 04/01/2006: Installed new version of <u>Qvm</u> (2.1.6), which fixed problem where <u>cache entries never got deleted.</u>
>
> 04/27/2006: If you use <u>KQED</u> version 6 or earlier, you have to rename the base directory to _kqed6 to avoid a conflict with the in-house <u>Core library.</u>

Figure 7.1: EXAMPLE OF A SOLUTIONS LOG ENTRY, WITH HYPERLINKS

Keep the log in a computer-searchable format. That way you can perform a keyword search to look up the details quickly. Figure 7.1 shows a simple example, with hyperlinks to more information.

When you face a problem and you can't find the solution in your log, remember to update your log with the new details as soon as you do figure out a solution.

Even better than maintaining a log is sharing it with others. Make it part of your shared network drive so others can use it. Or create a Wiki, and encourage other developers to use it and update it.

Maintain a log of problems and their solutions. *Part of fixing a problem is retaining details of the solution so you can find and apply it later.*

What It Feels Like

Your solutions log feels like part of your brain. You can find details on particular issues and also get guidance on similar but different issues.

Keeping Your Balance

- You still need to spend more time solving problems than documenting them. Keep it light and simple; it doesn't have to be publication quality.

- Finding previous solutions is critical; use plenty of keywords that will help you find an entry when needed.

- If a web search doesn't find *anyone* else with the same problem, perhaps you're using something incorrectly.

- Keep track of the specific version of the application, framework or platform where the problem occurred. The same problem can manifest itself differently on different platforms/versions.

- Record *why* the team made an important decision. That's the sort of detail that's hard to remember six to nine months later, when the decision needs to be revisited and recriminations fill the air.

Warnings Are Really Errors

"Compiler warnings are just for the overly cautious and pedantic. They're just warnings after all. If they were serious, they'd be errors, and you couldn't compile. So just ignore them, and let 'er rip."

When your program has a compilation error, the compiler or build tool refuses to produce an executable. You don't have a choice—you have to fix the error before moving on.

Warnings, unfortunately, are not like that. You can run the program that generates compiler warnings if you want. What happens if you ignore warnings and continue to develop your code? You're sitting on a ticking time bomb, one that will probably go off at the worst possible moment.

Some warnings are benign by-products of a fussy compiler (or interpreter), but others are not. For instance, a warning about a variable not being used in the code is probably benign but may also allude to the use of some other incorrect variable.

At a recent client site, Venkat found more than 300 warnings in an application in production. One of the warnings that was being ignored by the developers said this:

```
Assignment in conditional expression is always constant;
did you mean to use == instead of = ?
```

The offending code was something like this:

```
if (theTextBox.Visible = true)
...
```

In other words, that **if** will always evaluate as true, regardless of the hapless theTextBox variable. It's scary to see genuine errors such as this slip through as warnings and be ignored.

Consider the following C# code:

```
public class Base
{
  public virtual void foo()
  {
    Console.WriteLine("Base.foo");
  }
}
```

```
public class Derived : Base
{
  public virtual void foo()
  {
    Console.WriteLine("Derived.foo");
  }
}

class Test
{
  static void Main(string[] args)
  {
    Derived d = new Derived();
    Base b = d;
    d.foo();
    b.foo();
  }
}
```

When you compile this code using the default Visual Studio 2003 project settings, you'll see the message "Build: 1 succeeded, 0 failed, 0 skipped" at the bottom of the Output window. When you run the program, you'll get this output:

```
Derived.foo
Base.foo
```

But this isn't what you'd expect. You should see both the calls to foo() end up in the Derived class. What went wrong? If you examine the Output window closely, you'll find a warning message:

```
Warning. Derived.foo hides inherited member Base.foo
To make the current member override that implementation,
add the override keyword. Otherwise, you'd add the new keyword.
```

This was clearly an *error*—the code should use **override** instead of **virtual** in the Derived class's foo() method.[1] Imagine systematically ignoring warnings like this in your code. The behavior of your code becomes unpredictable, and its quality plummets.

You might argue that good unit tests will find these problems. Yes, they will help (and you should certainly use good unit tests). But if the compiler can detect this kind of problem, why not let it? It'll save you both some time and some headaches.

---

[1]And this is an insidious trap for former C++ programmers; the program would work as expected in C++.

Find a way to tell your compiler to treat warnings as errors. If your compiler allows you to fine-tune warning reporting levels, turn that knob all the way up so no warnings are ignored. GCC compilers support the -Werror flag, for example, and in Visual Studio, you can change the project settings to treat warnings as errors.

That is the least you should do on a project. Unfortunately, if you go that route, you will have to do it on each project you create. It'd be nice to enable that more or less globally.

In Visual Studio, for instance, you can modify the project templates (see *.NET Gotchas* [Sub05] for details) so any project you create on your machine will have the option set, and in the current version of Eclipse, you can change these settings under Window → Preferences → Java → Compiler → Errors/Warnings. If you're using other languages or IDEs, take time to find how you can treat warnings as errors in them.

While you're modifying settings, set those same flags in the continuous integration tool that you use on your build machine. (For details on continuous integration, see Practice 21, *Different Makes a Difference*, on page 90.) This small change can have a huge impact on the quality of the code that your team is checking into the source control system.

You want to get all of this set up right as you start the project; suddenly turning warnings on partway through a project may be too overwhelming to handle.

Just because your compiler treats warnings lightly doesn't mean you should.

> **Treat warnings as errors.** *Checking in code with warnings is just as bad as checking in code with errors or code that fails its tests. No checked-in code should produce any warnings from the build tools.*

What It Feels Like

Warnings feel like...well, warnings. They are warning you about something, and that gets your attention.

Keeping Your Balance

- Although we've been talking about compiled languages here, interpreted languages usually have a flag that enables run-time warnings. Use that flag, and capture the output so you can identify—and eliminate—the warnings.

- Some warnings can't be stopped because of compiler bugs or problems with third-party tools or code. If it can't be helped, don't waste further time on it. But this shouldn't happen very often.

- You can usually instruct the compiler to specifically suppress unavoidable warnings so you don't have to wade through them to find genuine warnings and errors.

- Deprecated methods have been deprecated for a reason. Stop using them. At a minimum, schedule an iteration where they (and their attendant warning messages) can be removed.

- If you mark methods you've written as deprecated, document what current users should do instead and when the deprecated methods will be removed altogether.

35 ▶ Attack Problems in Isolation

"Stepping line by line through a massive code base is pretty scary. But the only way to debug a significant problem is to look at the entire system. All at once. After all, you don't know where the problem may be, and that's the only way to find it."

One of the positive side effects of unit testing (Chapter 5, *Agile Feedback*, on page 79) is that it forces you to layer your code. To make your code testable, you have to untangle it from its surroundings. If your code depends on other modules, you'll use mock objects to isolate it from those other modules. In addition to making your code robust, it makes it easier to locate problems as they arise.

Otherwise, you may have problems figuring out where to even start. You might start by using a debugger, stepping through the code and trying to isolate the problem. You may have to go through a few forms or dialogs before you can get to the interesting part, and that makes it hard to reach the problem area. You may find yourself struggling with the entire system at this point, and that just increases stress and reduces productivity.

Large systems are complicated—many factors are involved in the way they execute. While working with the entire system, it's hard to separate the details that have an effect on your particular problem from the ones that don't.

The answer is clear: don't try to work with the whole system at once. Separate the component or module you're having problems with from the rest of the code base for serious debugging. If you have unit tests, you're there already. Otherwise, you'll have to get creative.

For instance, in the middle of a time-critical project (aren't they all?), Fred and George found themselves facing a major data corruption problem. It took a lot of work to find what was wrong, because their team didn't separate the database-related code from the rest of the application. They had no way to report the problem to the vendor—they certainly couldn't email the entire source code base to them!

So, they developed a small prototype that exhibited similar symptoms. They sent this to the vendor as an example and asked for their expert opinion. Working with the prototype helped them understand the issues more clearly.

Plus, if they *weren't* able to reproduce the problem in the prototype, it would have shown them examples of code that actually worked and would have helped them isolate the problem.

Prototype to isolate

The first step in identifying complex problems is to isolate them. You wouldn't try to fix an airplane engine in midair, so why would you diagnose a hard problem in a part or component of your application while it's working inside the entire application? It's easier to fix engines when they're out of the aircraft and on the workbench. Similarly, it's easier to fix problems in code if you can isolate the module causing the problem.

But many applications are written in a way that makes isolation difficult. Application components or parts may be intertwined with each other; try to extract one, and all the rest come along too.[2] In these cases, you may be better off spending some time ripping out the code that is of concern and creating a test bed on which to work.

Attacking a problem in isolation has a number of advantages: by isolating the problem from the rest of the application, you are able to focus directly on just the issues that are relevant to the problem. You can change as much as you need to get to the bottom of the problem—you aren't dealing with the live application. You get to the problem quicker because you're working with the minimal amount of relevant code.

Isolating problems is not just something you do after the application ships. Isolation can help us when prototyping, debugging, and testing.

 Attack problems in isolation. *Separate a problem area from its surroundings when working on it, especially in a large application.*

What It Feels Like

When faced with a problem that you have to isolate, it feels like searching for a needle in a tea cup, not a needle in a haystack.

---

[2]This is affectionately known as the "Big Ball of Mud" design antipattern.

Keeping Your Balance

- If you separate code from its environment and the problem goes away, you've helped to isolate the problem.

- On the other hand, if you separate code from its environment and the problem *doesn't* go away, you've still helped to isolate the problem.

- It can be useful to *binary chop* through a problem. That is, divide the problem space in half, and see which half contains the problem. Then divide that half in half again, and repeat.

- Before attacking your problem, consult your log (see Practice 33, *Keep a Solutions Log*, on page 132).

Report All Exceptions

"Protect your caller from weird exceptions. It's your job to handle it. Wrap everything you call, and send your own exception up instead—or just swallow it."

Part of any programming job is to think through how things should work. But it's much more profitable to think about what happens when things *don't* work—when things don't go as planned.

Perhaps you're calling some code that might throw an exception; in your own code you can try to handle and recover from that failure. It's great if you can recover and continue with the processing without your user being aware of any problem. If you can't recover, it's great to let the user of your code know exactly what went wrong.

But that doesn't always happen. Venkat found himself quite frustrated with a popular open-source library (which will remain unnamed here). When he invoked a method that was supposed to create an object, he received a null reference instead. The code was small, isolated, and simple enough, so not a whole lot could've been messed up at the code level. Still, he had no clue what went wrong.

Fortunately it was open source, so he downloaded the source code and examined the method in question. It in turn called another method, and that method determined that some necessary components were missing on his system. This low-level method threw an exception containing information to that effect. Unfortunately, the top-level method quietly suppressed that exception with an empty **catch** block and returned a null instead. The code Venkat had written had no way of knowing what had happened; only by reading the library code could he understand the problem and finally get the missing component installed.

Checked exceptions, such as those in Java, force you to catch or propagate exceptions. Unfortunately, some developers, maybe temporarily, catch and ignore exceptions just to keep the compiler from complaining. This is dangerous—temporary fixes are often forgotten and end up in production code. You must handle all exceptions and recover from the failures if you can. If you can't handle it yourself, propagate it to your method's caller so it can take a stab at handling it (or gracefully communicate the information about the problem to users; see Practice 37, *Provide Useful Error Messages*, on the next page).

Sounds pretty obvious, doesn't it? Well, maybe it's not as obvious as you think. A story in the news not long ago talked about a major failure of a large airline reservations system. The system crashed, grounding airplanes, stranding thousands of passengers, and snarling the entire air transportation system for days. The cause? *A single unchecked SQL exception in an application server.*

Maybe you'd enjoy the fame of being mentioned on CNN, but probably not like that.

 Handle or propagate all exceptions. *Don't suppress them, even temporarily. Write your code with the expectation that things will fail.*

What It Feels Like

You feel you can rely on getting an exception when something bad happens. There are no empty exception handlers.

Keeping Your Balance

- Determining who is responsible for handling an exception is part of design.

- Not all situations are exceptional.

- Report an exception that has meaning in the context of this code. A NullPointerException is pretty but just as useless as the **null** object described earlier.

- If the code writes a running debug log, issue a log message when an exception is caught or thrown; this will make tracking them down much easier.

- Checked exceptions can be onerous to work with. No one wants to call a method that throws thirty-one different checked exceptions. That's a design error: fix it, don't patch over it.

- Propagate what you can't handle.

Provide Useful Error Messages

"Don't scare the users, or even other programmers. Give them a nice, sanitized error message. Use something comforting like 'User Error. Replace, and Continue.'"

As applications are deployed and put into use in the real world, things will fail from time to time. A computation module may fail, for instance, or the connection to a database server may be lost. When you can't honor a user's request, you want to handle it gracefully.

When such an error occurs, is it enough to pop up a graceful, apologetic message to the user? Sure, a general message that informs the user about a failure is better than the application misbehaving or disappearing because of a crash (which leaves the user confused and wondering what happened). However, a message along the lines of "something went wrong" doesn't help your team diagnose the problem. When users call your support team to report the problem, you'd like them to report a lot of good information so you can identify the problem quickly. Unfortunately, with just a general error message, they won't be able to tell you much.

The most common solution to this issue is logging: when something goes wrong, have the application log details of the error. In the most rudimentary approach, the log is maintained as a text file. But you might instead publish to a systemwide event log. You can use tools to browse through the logs, generate an RSS feed of all logged messages, and so on.

While logging is useful, it is not sufficient: it might give you, the developer, information if you dig for it, but it doesn't help the hapless user. If you show them something like the message in Figure 7.2, on the facing page, they are left clueless—they don't know what they did wrong, what they might do to work around it, or even what to report when they call tech support.

If you pay attention, you may find early warning signs of this problem during development. As a developer, you'll often pretend to be a user in order to test new functionality. If error messages are hard for you to understand or are not helpful to locate problems, imagine how hard it will be for your real users and your support team.

Figure 7.2: EXCEPTION MESSAGE THAT DOESN'T HELP

For example, suppose the logon UI calls the middle tier of your application, which makes a request to its database tier. The database tier throws an exception because it couldn't connect to a database. The middle tier then wraps that exception into its own exception and passes that up. What should your UI tier do? It should at least let the user know there was a system error, and it's not due to any user input.

So the user calls up and tells you that he can't log on. How can you locate the actual problem? The log file may have hundreds of entries, and it's going to be hard to find the relevant details.

Instead, provide more details right in the message you give the user. Imagine being able to see exactly which SQL query or stored procedure messed up: this can make the difference between finding the problem and moving ahead versus wasting hours trying to find the problem blindly. On the other hand, providing the specific details about what went wrong during database connectivity doesn't help the users once the application is in production. It may well scare the living daylights out of some users.

On one hand, you want to provide users with a clean, high-level explanation of what went wrong so that they can understand the problem and perhaps pursue a workaround. On the other hand, you want to give them all the low-level, nitty-gritty details of the error so that you can identify the real problem in the code.

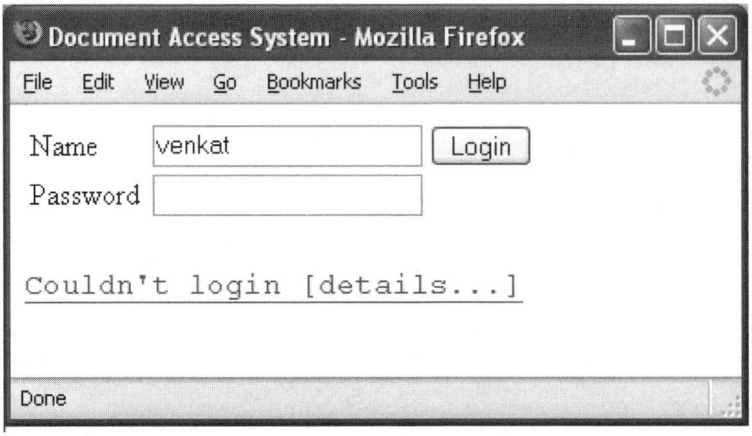

Figure 7.3: AN EXCEPTION MESSAGE WITH LINK FOR MORE DETAILS

Here's one way to reconcile those disparate goals: Figure 7.3 shows a high-level message that appears when something goes wrong. This error message, instead of being just simple text, contains a hyperlink. The user, the developers, or the testers can then follow this link to get more information, as shown in Figure 7.4, on the facing page.

When you follow the link, you'll see details about the exception (and all the nested exceptions). During development, you may want to simply display these details by default. When the application goes into production, however, you'll probably want to modify this so that instead of displaying these gory details directly to the users, you provide a link or some sort of handle or entry into your error log. Your support team can ask the user to click the error message and read the handle so they can quickly find the specific details in the log. In the case of a stand-alone system, clicking the link might email the details of what went wrong directly to your support department.

The information you've logged may contain not only the details about what went wrong but also a snapshot of the state of the system as well (the session state in a web application, for example).[3]

---

[3]Some security-sensitive information should not be revealed or even logged; this includes items such as passwords, account numbers, etc.

Figure 7.4: Complete details displayed for debugging

Using these details, your support group can re-create the situation that caused the problem, which will really help efforts to find and fix the issue.

Error reporting has a big impact on developer productivity as well as your eventual support costs. If finding and fixing problems during development is frustrating, take it as an early sign that you need a more proactive approach to error reporting. Debugging information is precious and hard to come by. Don't throw it away.

 Present useful error messages. *Provide an easy way to find the details of errors. Present as much supporting detail as you can about a problem when it occurs, but don't bury the user with it.*

Distinguishing Types of Errors

Program defects. These are genuine bugs, such as NullPointer-Exception, missing key values, etc. There's nothing the user or system administrators can do.

Environmental problems. This category includes failure to connect to a database or a remote web service, a full disk, insufficient permissions, and that sort of thing. The programmer can't do anything about it, but the user might be able to get around it, and the system administrator certainly should be able to fix it, if you give them sufficiently detailed information.

User error. No need to bother the programmer or the system administrators about this; the user just needs to try again, after you tell them what they did wrong.

By keeping track of what kind of error you are reporting, you can provide more appropriate advice to your audience.

What It Feels Like

Error messages feel useful and helpful. When a problem arises, you can hone in on the precise details of what went wrong, where.

Keeping Your Balance

- An error message that says "File Not Found" is not helpful by itself. "Can't open /andy/project/main.yaml for reading" is much more informative.

- You don't have to wait for an exception to tell you something went wrong. Use assertions at key points in the code to make sure everything is correct. When an assertion fails, provide the same good level of detail you would for exception reporting.

- Providing more information should not compromise security, privacy, trade secrets, or any other sensitive information (this is especially true for web-based applications).

- The information you provide the user might include a key to help you find the relevant section in a log file or audit trail.

I not only use all of the brains I have, but
all I can borrow.
▶ Woodrow Wilson, U.S. president

Chapter 8

Agile Collaboration

Any nontrivial project requires a team of people. The days of building a full product alone, in your garage, have pretty much passed us by. But working in a team is very different from working alone; suddenly, your actions have consequences on the productivity and progress of others in the team and on the entire project.

The success of a project depends on how effectively the people on the team work together, how they interact, and how they manage their activities. Everyone's actions must be relevant to the context of the project, and in turn each individual action affects the project context.

Effective collaboration is a cornerstone of agile development, and these practices will help keep everyone involved and headed in the right direction—together.

The first step you want to take is to *Schedule Regular Face Time*, on page 151. A face-to-face meeting is still the most effective way to communicate, so we'll start with that. Next, you want to get everyone in the game. That means *Architects Must Write Code* (we'll see why on page 155). And since you and your team are all in this together, you want to *Practice Collective Ownership* (that's on page 158) to make sure you aren't held hostage by any one team member. This is a collaborative effort, remember?

But effective collaboration is more than just banging code out the door. Everyone on the team needs to refine and improve their skills over time and grow their careers. Even if you're just starting out, you can *Be a Mentor*, and we'll see how on page 160. Many times you'll know the answer to something that a teammate may not know. You can help grow the team if you *Allow People to Figure It Out*, as we'll see on page 163.

Finally, since you are working together on a team, you need to modify some of your personal coding practices to accommodate the rest of the team. For starters, it's polite to *Share Code Only When Ready* (starting on page 165) so as not to encumber your teammates with half-baked works in progress. When you're ready, you'll want to *Review Code* with other team members (and we'll look at that on page 168). As the project rolls along and you complete tasks and take on new ones, you need to *Keep Others Informed* about your progress, problems you've encountered, and neat things you've discovered. We'll conclude with that practice on page 171.

Schedule Regular Face Time

"You need to hold meetings—lots of them. In fact, we're going to keep scheduling more meetings until we discover why no work is getting done."

You may personally hate meetings, but communication is key to the success of projects. Not only do you need to talk to your customers, but you must interact well with fellow developers. You certainly want to know what others are doing—if Bernie has a solution to the problem that you are struggling with, you'd like to know about it sooner rather than later, right?

Stand-up meetings (introduced in Scrum and emphasized in XP) are an effective way to get the team together and keep everyone informed. As the name suggests, participants aren't allowed to sit down in stand-up meetings. This helps keep the meetings short; you might get too comfortable when you sit down, and as a result meetings tend to go on forever.

Andy once had a client where he and Dave Thomas participated in the stand-up meeting remotely via speakerphone. Things were going very well until one day the meeting suddenly lasted twice as long as usual. You guessed it; they had moved into a conference room and were sitting down in comfy armchairs.

A seated meeting usually lasts longer; most people generally don't like to continue long conversations standing up.

To help keep the meeting focused, everyone should limit their contribution to answering these three questions:

- What did I achieve yesterday?
- What am I planning to do today?
- What's in my way?

Each participant is given only a short amount of time to talk (about two minutes). You may want to have a timer to help those of us who have the tendency to ramble. If you want to discuss something in greater detail, then get together with the appropriate people after the stand-up meeting (it's OK to say, "I need to talk to Fred and Wilma about the database" during the meeting; just don't start going into the details).

> ### Pigs and Chickens
>
> Scrum names the roles of team members versus nonteam members as *pigs* and *chickens*. Team members are pigs (there goes the self-esteem!) and nonteam members (managers, support, QA, etc.) are chickens. The terms come from a fable of barnyard animals getting together to open a restaurant. When planning to serve bacon and eggs for breakfast, the chicken is certainly involved, but the pigs are *committed*.
>
> Only "pigs" are allowed to participate in the Scrum stand-up meeting.

The stand-up meeting is usually held early in the day when everyone is at work. Don't schedule this as the very first thing; you have to give everyone a chance to make it through the traffic, get some coffee and delete the latest spam scam emails and other unsolicited, salacious offers. You need to get the meeting over with in time to get a good amount of work done before lunch, but you don't want it so early that everyone is coffee-deprived and groggy. Thirty minutes to an hour after the nominal arrival time is probably a good target.

Those who attend the meeting follow a few rules in order to stay on track and keep the focus of the meeting: only team members—developers, product owner, and coordinator—can speak (see the description of "pigs" versus "chickens" in the sidebar). They have to answer the three questions and should not get into lengthy discussions (but it's OK to arrange to talk later). The manager jots down the list of issues to resolve and shouldn't try to direct the conversation other than keeping people focused on the three questions.

Stand-up meetings provide many benefits:

- They kick off the day ahead in a focused way.

- If a developer is having problems with something, he or she has an opportunity to bring the issue out into the open and actively seek help.

- They help determine areas that may need additional hands and allow for team leads or managers to obtain or reassign people.

Using a Kitchen Timer

Developer Nancy Davis tells us about her experience using a kitchen timer for her team's stand-up meetings:

"We used a kitchen timer my sister gave me for Christmas last year. It didn't make a low *clicking* noise while running, and it made just one ding at the end. If the timer went off, we just added two minutes and went on to the next person. Occasionally, we just forgot the timer and went as long as we needed, but mostly we stuck with it."

- They make team members aware of what's going on in other areas of the project.

- They help you quickly identify redundancy or areas where someone else has a solution.

- They speed development by facilitating the sharing of code and ideas.

- They encourage forward momentum: seeing others report progress motivates each of us to do the same.

Carrying out stand-up meetings requires commitment and participation from management. However, lead developers in a team can be instrumental in getting this started. When developers can't get management to participate, they can hold stand-up meetings among themselves informally.

 Use stand-up meetings. *Stand-up meetings keep the team on the same page. Keep the meeting short, focused, and intense.*

What It Feels Like

You look forward to the stand-up meeting. You get a good sense of what everyone else is working on and can bring problems out into the open easily.

Keeping Your Balance

- Meetings take time away from development, so you need to maximize the return on investment of your time. Stand-up meetings should never take more than thirty minutes maximum, and ten to fifteen minutes is a realistic target.

- If you're using a conference room that has to be reserved, reserve it for a full hour. That gives you an opportunity to use it immediately for smaller meetings after the fifteen-minute stand-up has ended.

- Although most teams need to meet every day, for small teams that might be overkill. Meeting every other day, or twice a week, may be sufficient.

- Watch the level of detail being reported. You need to report concrete progress during the meeting, but don't get bogged down in low-level details. For instance, "I'm working on the logon screen" is not sufficient. "Logon accepts the user name and password of *guest/guest* and I'll hook up to the database tomorrow" is about the right level of detail.

- Part of keeping a short meeting short is starting promptly. Don't waste time waiting to get the meeting started.

- If the stand-up meeting feels like a waste of time, perhaps you aren't really operating as a team. That's not necessarily a bad thing as long as you're aware of it.

39 ▶ Architects Must Write Code

"Fred, our expert architect, will deliver a design for you to code. He's very experienced and very expensive, so don't waste his time with silly questions or implementation problems."

The industry is full of people with the title Software Architect. It's a title your authors don't like much, and here's why: an *architect* is a person who designs and guides, but many of

You can't code in PowerPoint

the people with Architect on their business cards don't deserve the title. An architect is not a person who just draws pretty pictures, speaks jargon, and uses lots of patterns—such designers are often ineffective.

They typically come in during the beginning of a project, draw all kinds of diagrams, and leave before any serious implementation takes place. There are many "PowerPoint architects" out there, and they aren't effective because of lack of feedback.

A design is specific to the problem at hand, and your understanding of the problem changes as you implement that design. It's hard to come up with an effective detailed design up front (see Practice 11, *Let Design Guide, Not Dictate*, on page 50): there isn't enough context, and there's little or no feedback. Design evolves over time; you can't design a new feature, or an enhancement, by ignoring the realities of the application (its implementation).

As a designer, you can't be even marginally effective without understanding the nitty-gritty details of the system. You don't get this kind of understanding working solely with high-level diagrams.

It's like trying to conduct a battle from miles away by looking only at the map—once the battle begins, planning is not sufficient. Strategic decisions may be made from miles away, but tactical decisions—decisions that determine victory or defeat—require significant understanding of what's on the ground.[1]

---

[1] In World War I, the Battle of the Somme was intended to be a decisive breakthrough. Instead, it became the greatest military folly of the twentieth century, mostly because of a loss of communication and the way the commanders insisted on following the plan even when facing a very different reality. See http://www.worldwar1.com/sfsomme.htm.

> ### Reversibility
>
> *The Pragmatic Programmer* (HT00) points out *There Are No Final Decisions.* No decision you make should be cast in stone. Instead, consider each major decision about as permanent as a sandcastle at the beach and explicitly plan ahead for change.

Designer of a new system
by Donald E. Knuth

> The designer of a new kind of system must participate fully in the implementation.

As Knuth says, a good designer is someone who can roll up his sleeves and get his hands dirty, coding without hesitation. A true architect would protest mightily if told they couldn't be involved in the code.

A Tamil proverb suggests that "A picture of a vegetable doesn't make good curry." Similarly, a paper design will not make a good application. Design should be prototyped, tested, and validated as well—it has to evolve. It's the responsibility of the designer, or the architect, to realize a design that actually works.

Martin Fowler, in his article entitled "Who Needs an Architect?"[2] says that the role of a real architect "...is to mentor the development team, to raise their level so that they can take on more complex issues." He goes on to say, "I think that one of an architect's most important tasks is to remove architecture by finding ways to eliminate irreversibility in software designs." Fostering *reversibility* is a key component of the pragmatic approach (see the sidebar on this page).

Encourage your programmers to design. A lead programmer may take the role of an architect—and may indeed wear different hats. This person is immersed in design issues, but not at the expense of giving up coding. If developers are reluctant to take on these design responsibilities, pair them with someone who can design well. A programmer who refuses to design is a person who refuses to think.

---

[2]http://www.martinfowler.com/ieeeSoftware/whoNeedsArchitect.pdf

Good design evolves from active programmers. *Real insight comes from active coding. Don't use architects who don't code—they can't design without knowing the realities of your system.*

What It Feels Like

Architecture, design, coding, and testing feel like different facets of the same activity—development. They shouldn't feel like separate activities.

Keeping Your Balance

- If you have one chief architect, he or she may not have enough time to be a full-fledged coder as well. Keep them involved but not on the critical path on the largest piece of code.

- Don't let anyone design in isolation, especially yourself.

40 ► Practice Collective Ownership

"Don't worry about that crippling bug; Joe will fix it when he gets back from vacation next week. Just work around it until then."

Any nontrivial application requires collaborative effort to develop. In that context, there's no good reason to take territorial ownership of code. Any team members who understand a piece of code should be able to work on it. You increase risk by keeping a piece of code exclusively in the hands of a single developer.

Solving problems and making the application meet its users' expectations are more important than deciding who has the most brilliant idea, or, for that matter, whose implementation stinks.

When multiple people work with code, the code is constantly checked, refactored, and maintained. If a fix is needed, any one of the developers can pitch in to get the work done. Project scheduling becomes easier when more than one person can comfortably work with different parts of your application code.

You'll find that the overall knowledge and experience level of the people in the team improves when you rotate them through tasks, giving them the opportunity to work with different parts of the application. When Joe picks up code that Sally wrote, he may refactor it, ironing out issues that need attention. He will ask useful questions while trying to understand the code, providing significant early insight into problems.

From the other side, knowing that others are going to work on your code means you'll be more disciplined. You have to be more careful if you know others are watching.

You might argue that if a developer is exclusively assigned to work on one area, then he is going to be highly proficient in it, leading to faster development. That's true, but in the long term, you gain benefits by having multiple eyes look at a piece of code. It helps improve the overall quality of the code, it's easier to maintain and understand, and the errors decrease.

Emphasize collective ownership of code. *Rotate develop-ers across different modules and tasks in different areas of the system.*

What It Feels Like

You feel comfortable working on most any part of the project.

Keeping Your Balance

- Don't accidentally lose expertise on your team. If one developer is highly skilled in an area, it may be advantageous to keep them as the resident expert in that subject while still exposing them to the rest of the system.

- In a large project it can get very messy if everyone randomly changes everything all the time. Collective ownership is not a license to hack wildly.

- You don't need to know every detail of every part of the project, but you shouldn't be scared away from any part of the system either.

- There are special occasions when you don't want collective own-ership. Perhaps the code requires specialized, specific problem-domain knowledge, such as in a hard real-time control system. In these cases, you may find that too many cooks spoil the broth.

- People *do* occasionally get run over by buses or suffer other sud-den calamities, including getting hired by the competition. When you don't share knowledge on the team, you risk losing it entirely.

Be a Mentor

"It took you a long time and a lot of hard work to get where you are. Keep it to yourself so you look better. Use your superior skills to intimidate your teammates."

There may come a time when you realize that you know more about some particular subject than others in your team. What can you do with this newfound authority? Well, you could use it to criticize others, making fun of decisions they make and code they write—we've certainly seen folks who do just that. Alternatively, you could share what you know, making those around you better.

Knowledge grows when given

"And no matter how many people share it, the idea is not diminished. When I hear your idea, I gain knowledge without diminishing anything of yours. In the same way, if you use your candle to light mine, I get light without darkening you. Like fire, ideas can encompass the globe without lessening their density."[3]

Working with others on a team is a great learning experience. Knowledge has several unique properties; if you give someone money, for instance, you end up with less and they end up with more. But if you educate someone, both of you gain more knowledge.

By taking the time to explain what you know, you get a better understanding of it yourself. You also get a different perspective when someone asks you questions. You might find yourself picking up a few new tips and tricks—you may hear yourself say, "I hadn't thought about it that way before."

By engaging with others, you motivate them to better themselves, which improves the overall competence of your team. And questions that you can't answer point out areas where you may not be as strong—where you need to focus further in order to improve. A good mentor takes notes while offering advice to others. You'll stop to jot down topics you want to spend more time looking at or thinking about. Add these notes to your daylog (see Practice 33, *Keep a Solutions Log*, on page 132).

---

[3]Thomas Jefferson

Being a mentor doesn't mean you spend all your time holding team members' hands and spoon-feeding them information (see Practice 42, *Allow People to Figure It Out*, on page 163). It doesn't mean you have to lecture at a white board or give quizzes. You might decide to present at a brown-bag lunch, but mostly being a mentor means helping your fellow teammates improve their game as well as helping yourself.

And you don't have to stop at the borders of your team. Start a personal blog, and post something code or technology related on it. It doesn't have to be an epic work; even a small code snippet and explanation might be useful to someone.

Being a mentor means sharing—not hoarding—what you know. It means taking an interest in seeing others learn and develop and adding increasing value to the team. It's all about building up your teammates and yourself, not about tearing down.

Unfortunately, it seems to be part of human nature to struggle up the ladder and then look down on others with disdain. Perhaps without even realizing it, it's easy to create a communication barrier. Others in the team either may begin to fear you or may be too embarrassed to approach you with questions. Then there's no exchange of knowledge. Being such an expert is like having great wealth and not having the health to enjoy it. You want to be a mentor, not a tormenter.

 Be a mentor. *There's fun in sharing what you know—you gain as you give. You motivate others to achieve better results. You improve the overall competence of your team.*

What It Feels Like

You find that teaching is another way to improve your own learning, and others come to trust that you can help them.

Keeping Your Balance

- If you keep teaching the same topics over and over to different people, keep notes to write an article or a book about the subject.

- Being a mentor is a great way to invest in your team (see Practice 6, *Invest in Your Team*, on page 32).

- Pair programming (see Practice 44, *Review Code*, on page 168) is a natural environment for effective mentoring.

- If you find yourself getting interrupted by people who seem too lazy to find the answer for themselves, see Practice 42, *Allow People to Figure It Out*, on the next page.

- Set a time limit for how long anyone on the team can be stuck on a problem before asking for help. One hour seems to be a pretty good target.

42 ▶ Allow People to Figure It Out

"You're so smart; just provide neat solutions to others on the team. Don't waste time trying to educate them."

"Give a man a fish, and you'll feed him for a day. Teach him to fish, and you will feed him for a lifetime." And he won't bother you again for weeks. Part of being a good mentor involves teaching your teammates to fish, not just handing them a fish every day.

After reading *Be a Mentor*, you may be inclined to dispatch a co-worker with a quick answer and get on with the task. But what happens if you just give them pointers and let the developer figure out their own answer?

This doesn't have to be a big deal; instead of answering something obvious like "42," ask your teammate, "Did you look at the interaction between the transaction manager and the application lock handler?"

Using this technique has a few advantages:

- You are helping them learn how to approach the problem.

- They get to learn more than just the answer.

- They won't keep coming to you with similar questions again and again.

- You are helping them function when you are not available to answer questions.

- They may come back with solutions or ideas you didn't consider. This is the fun part—you learn something new as well.

If the person comes back empty-handed, you can always supply more hints (or even the answer). If the person returns with some ideas, you can help them evaluate the pros and cons of each idea. If the person returns with a *better* answer or solution than what you had thought of, you can learn from the experience and share your thoughts. This serves as a great educational experience for both of you.

As a mentor, you lead others toward solutions, motivating them to solve problems and giving them an opportunity to think and learn problem solving. We mentioned Aristotle's quote earlier: "It is the mark of an educated mind to be able to entertain a thought without accepting it." You are entertaining thoughts and perspectives of others, and in the process you broaden yours.

When the whole team adopts that attitude, you'll find that the intellectual capital of the team increases rapidly, and you can start creating some really great stuff.

Give others a chance to solve problems. *Point them in the right direction instead of handing them solutions. Everyone can learn something in the process.*

What It Feels Like

It feels like you are being helpful without spoon-feeding. You're not cryptic or cagey, but you can lead people to find their own answers.

Keeping Your Balance

- Answer the question with another question that leads in the right direction.

- If someone is truly stuck, don't torment them. Show them the answer, and explain why it's the answer.

43 ▶ Share Code Only When Ready

"Check in all code as often as you can, especially when you leave for the day, whether it's ready or not."

Here's a riddle for you: what's worse than not using a version control system? Answer: using it incorrectly. The way you use version control can affect productivity, product stability, quality, and schedules. In particular, something as simple as how often you check in your code makes a big difference.

You should check in code as soon as you are done with a task; you don't want to hold that code on your computer for an extended period of time. What good is your code if you have not made it available for others to integrate and use? You need to get it out to start getting feedback.[4]

Obviously, checking in code weekly or monthly is not desirable—you're not using version control for its intended purpose. You might hear various excuses for such sloppy habits. Maybe folks say that developers are working off-site or offshore and the access to the version control system is very slow. This is an example of *environmental viscosity*—it's easier to do the wrong thing than to do the right thing. Clearly that's a simple technical problem that needs to be addressed.

On the other hand, how about checking in the code before you are done with the task? Perhaps you are working on some critical code, and you want to go home and work on it after dinner. The easiest way to get to this code at home is to check it into version control system at work and check it out when you get home.

But if you check in code you are still working on, you're putting the code into the repository in an unworkable state. It might have compilation errors, or the changes you have made might not be compatible with the rest of the code in the system. Now you're affecting other developers as soon as they fetch the latest copy of the code.

Normally, you check in a group of files that relate to a specific task or a bug you have fixed. You check them all in together, along with a

---

[4]Plus, you don't want to keep the only copy of the code on a hard drive backed only by a "ninety-day limited warranty" for very long.

> ### Safe, But Not Checked In
>
> If you need to transfer or save source code that isn't quite done yet, you have a couple of options:
>
> **Use remote access.** Instead of checking in half-baked code to take it home, leave the code at work, and use remote access to work on it.
>
> **Take it with you.** Copy the code to a USB stick, CD, or DVD to work on off-site.
>
> **Use a docking laptop.** If this is a persistent problem, perhaps you could use a laptop with a docking station; that way you could have the code with you anywhere.
>
> **Use version control features.** Microsoft Visual Team System 2005 has a "shelving" feature, some products have the notion of promoting code to be available to others independent of checking it in to the system, and in CVS and Subversion you can set up developer branches for code that isn't ready for the main line (see (TH03) and (Mas05)).

meaningful log message that will let folks in the future figure out what files changed and, more important, why. This kind of atomic commit will also help should you need to roll back the change.

Make sure all your unit tests still pass before checking in the code. One easy way for you to make sure the code in the control system is healthy is to use continuous integration.

Share code only when ready. *Never check in code that's not ready for others. Deliberately checking in code that doesn't compile or pass its unit tests should be considered an act of criminal project negligence.*

What It Feels Like

You feel the team sitting there at the other end of the version control system. You know that as soon you check in, the world has it.

Keeping Your Balance

- Some version control systems distinguish between "checked-in" and "publicly available." In that case, you can perform temporary check-ins (while traveling between home and work, for example) without incurring the wrath of your teammates.

- Some people like to require code reviews before allowing code to be checked in. That's fine, as long as it doesn't unduly delay the check-in. If any part of your process is slowing you down, revise your process.

- You still need to check in code frequently. Don't use "it's not ready" as an excuse to avoid checking in code.

Review Code

"Users make great testers. Don't worry—if it's wrong, they'll tell us eventually."

The best time to find problems in code is as soon as the code is written. If you let code sit and rot for a while, it won't smell any prettier.

Code Reviews and Defect Removal
by Capers Jones in Estimating Software Costs [Jon98]

> Formal code inspections are about twice as efficient as any known form of testing in finding deep and obscure programming bugs and are the only known method to top 80 percent in defect-removal efficiency.

As Capers Jones points out, code reviews are probably the best single way to locate and solve problems. Unfortunately, it's sometimes hard to convince managers and developers to use them.

Managers worry about the time it takes to review the code. They don't want their team to quit coding and get into lengthy code review meetings. Developers fear code reviews; they feel threatened by others looking at their code. It affects their egos. They are worried about being emotionally beaten up.

On projects where your authors have practiced code reviews, the results have been remarkable.

Venkat recently worked on a very aggressively scheduled project with some less experienced developers. They were able to deliver top-quality and stable code by using rigorous code reviews. When developers on the team completed their coding and testing of a task, the code was thoroughly reviewed by another developer before it was even checked in to version control.

Quite a few problems were fixed in this process. Oh, and code reviews are not just for code written by junior developers—you should perform code reviews on the code written by every developer in the team, regardless of their experience.

So how do you review code? You can choose from a couple of different basic styles.

The all-nighter. You could hold a one-night-a-month monster code review session, bring your entire team together, and order pizza. But this may not be the most effective way to hold code reviews (and doesn't sound particularly agile). Large review teams tend to get into lengthy and extended discussions. Such a broad review may not only be unnecessary, but it might even be detrimental to progress. We don't recommend this style.

The pick-up game. As soon as some code has been written, compiled, tested, and is ready for check-in, the code is picked up for review by another developer. These "commit reviews" are designed to be a quick, low-ceremony way to make sure the code is acceptable before checking it in. In order to eliminate any behavioral ruts, try to rotate through developers. For instance, if Jane reviewed Joey's code last time, ask Mark to review it this time. This can be a very effective technique.[5]

Pair programming. In Extreme Programming, you never code alone. Code is always written in pairs: one person sits at the keyboard (the *driver*), and one person sits back and acts as *navigator*. Every so often, they switch roles. Having a second pair of eyes acts like a continuous code review; you don't have to schedule any separate, specific review time.

What should you look for during a code review? You might develop your own list of specific issues to check (all exception handlers are nonempty, all database calls are made within the scope of a transaction, and so on), but here's a very minimal list to get you started:

- Can you read and understand the code?

- Are there any obvious errors?

- Will the code have any undesirable effect on other parts of the application?

- Is there any duplication of code (within this section of code itself or with other parts of the system)?

- Are there any reasonable improvements or refactorings that can improve it?

---

[5]For more details on this style, see *Ship It!* [RG05].

In addition, you might want to consider using code analysis tools such as Similarity Analyzer or Jester. If that sort of static analysis proves useful to you, make these tools part of your continuous build.

 Review all code. *Code reviews are invaluable in improving the quality of the code and keeping the error rate low. If done correctly, reviews can be practical and effective. Review code after each task, using different developers.*

What It Feels Like

Code reviews happen in small chunks, continuously. It feels like an ongoing part of the project, not a big scary event.

Keeping Your Balance

- Rubber-stamp code reviews without thought are without value.

- Code reviews need to actively evaluate the design and clarity of the code, not just whether the variable names and layout are compliant to some corporate standard.

- Different developers may write the same code quite differently. Different is not necessarily worse. Don't criticize code unless you can make it measurably better.

- Code reviews are useless unless you follow up on the recommendations quickly. You can schedule a follow-up meeting or use a system of code annotations to mark what needs to be done and track that it has been handled.

- Always close the loop on code reviewers; let everyone know what steps you took as a result of the review.

45 Keep Others Informed

"The manager, your team, and the business owners are relying on you to get tasks done. If they want your status, they'll ask you for it. Just keep your head down, and keep working."

By accepting a task, you have agreed to deliver it on time. But, it's not unusual to run into problems and face delays. The deadline arrives and at the demo you are expected to show the code working. What if you arrive at the meeting and inform everyone that you haven't finished? Besides being embarrassing, it's not healthy for your career.

If you wait until the deadline to deliver bad news, you're just begging your manager and technical lead to micromanage you. They'll be worried that you'll surprise them again so will check with you several times a day to make sure you are progressing. Your life is now evolving into a *Dilbert* cartoon.

Suppose you are in the middle of a task. It looks as if technical difficulties mean you won't be able to finish it on time. If you take the proactive step of informing others, you are giving them an opportunity to help figure out a solution ahead of time. Maybe they can ask another developer to help. They may reassign the task to someone else who may be more familiar with it. They may help you by giving more input on what needs to be done, or they may adjust the scope of work to what's doable in this iteration. Your customer may be willing to trade the task with some other equally important task.

By keeping others informed, you eliminate surprises, and they are comfortable they know your progress. They know when to provide you with helping hands, and you've earned their trust.

A traditional way to keep people informed is to send them an email, send them a message on a sticky note, or make a quick phone call. Another way to is to use what Alistair Cockburn calls "information radiators."[6] An information radiator is something like a poster on the wall providing information that changes over time. Passersby pick up the information effortlessly. By pushing the information at them, you eliminate the need for them to ask you questions. Your information

---

[6]See http://c2.com/cgi-bin/wiki?InformationRadiator.

radiators can display the progress you are making on your tasks and any additional information you think will be of interest to your team, manager, or customers.

You might use a poster on the wall, a website or Wiki, or a blog or RSS feed. As long as you put the information somewhere that people will look at *regularly*, then you're in the right place.

The whole team can use information radiators to broadcast their status, code designs, cool new ideas they've researched, and so on. Now just by walking around you can get smarter, and your manager will know exactly what's up.

Keep others informed. *Publish your status, your ideas and the neat things you're looking at. Don't wait for others to ask you the status of your work.*

What It Feels Like

You don't feel pestered by managers or co-workers constantly asking for your status or your latest design or research efforts.

Keeping Your Balance

- The daily stand-up meeting (see Practice 38, *Schedule Regular Face Time*, on page 151) helps keep everyone up-to-date at a high level.

- When presenting status, make sure the level of detail is appropriate for the audience. CEOs and business owners don't care about obscure details of abstract base classes, for instance.

- Don't spend more time or effort keeping others informed than actually getting your work done.

- Stay head's up, not head down.

As one lamp serves to dispel a thousand years of darkness, so one flash of wisdom destroys ten thousand years of ignorance.

▶ Hui-Neng

Chapter 9

Epilogue: Moving to Agility

One flash of wisdom. That's all it takes. We hope you've enjoyed our description of these agile practices and that at least one or two will serve to spark that flash of wisdom for you.

No matter what your experience has been so far, whether it has been highly successful or somewhat challenged, just one new practice can blow away any cobwebs and make a real difference to your career and your life. You can use a subset of these practices to rescue a project in trouble, or you can plan to introduce a fuller set over time.

9.1 Just One New Practice

For example, consider this story of one of Andy's former clients. The team had beautiful offices lined up in a graceful curve along the outside wall of a towering glass office building. Everyone had a window view, and the entire team ringed about half of the building. But there were problems. Releases were running late, and bugs were escalating out of control.

So in the usual fashion, the Pragmatic Programmers started on one end of the offices and began interviewing the team to find out what they were working on, what was working well, and what things were in the way. The first fellow explained that they were building a client-server application, with a razor-thin client and a fat server containing all the business logic and database access.

But as the interviewing progressed down the long line of offices, the story slowly changed. The vision of the project drifted a little bit with each person. Finally, the last person at the end of the line proudly explained the system as being a *fat* client, containing all the GUI and business logic, with nothing on the server except a simple database!

It became clear that the team never got together to talk about the project; instead, each team member only ever talked to the person immediately next to them. Just as in a school kid's game of "telephone," the message inevitably gets corrupted and distorted as it passes from person to person.

The pragmatic advice? Start using the stand-up meeting immediately (see Practice 38, *Schedule Regular Face Time*, on page 151). The results were fast and amazing. Not only did the architectural issues get quickly resolved, but something deeper happened. The team began to jell— began to form a cohesive unit, working together. Bug rates fell, the product became more stable, and deadlines weren't as deadly.

It didn't take long, and it didn't take a lot of effort. It required some discipline to stick with the meeting, but even that soon became a habit. It was just *one new practice,* but it made a huge difference to the team.

9.2 Rescuing a Failing Project

So if one practice is good, then all of them must be better, right? Eventually, yes, but not all at once—and especially not if the project is already in trouble. Changing *all* your development practices on a project at once is the best way to kill it.

To use a medical analogy, suppose you have a patient with chest pain. Of course, if the patient exercised regularly and ate well, they wouldn't be in trouble. But you can't just say, "Get your butt off the bed, and start running on the treadmill." That would be fatal and surely cause your malpractice insurance rates to rise.

You have to stabilize the patient using the minimum (but essential) medicines and procedures. Only once the patient is stable can you offer a regime to maintain good health.

When a project is failing, you'll want to introduce a couple of practices to stabilize the situation first. For example, Venkat once got a panicked call from a prospective client; their project was in shambles. They had spent half their allotted time and still had 90% of the project to deliver.

The manager was unhappy that the developers did not produce enough code fast enough. The developers were unhappy that the manager was pushing too hard. Should they spend the rest of the day fixing bugs or writing new functionality? Despite the depth of the crisis, the team was genuinely interested in succeeding. But they didn't know how. Everything they did put them further behind. They felt threatened and weren't comfortable making decisions.

Instead of trying to fix everything all at once, Venkat had to first stabilize the patient, starting with communication and collaboration-oriented practices such as Practice 3, *Criticize Ideas, Not People*, on page 19; Practice 38, *Schedule Regular Face Time*, on page 151; Practice 43, *Share Code Only When Ready*, on page 165; and Practice 45, *Keep Others Informed*, on page 171. From there, the next step was to introduce simple release practices such as Practice 13, *Keep It Releasable*, on page 57, and Practice 14, *Integrate Early, Integrate Often*, on page 60. Finally, they started a few helpful coding practices such as Practice 34, *Warnings Are Really Errors*, on page 135, and Practice 35, *Attack Problems in Isolation*, on page 139. It was enough to avert the crisis; the project was completed two weeks ahead of schedule and received acclaim from higher-level managers.

That's the emergency rescue model. If things aren't that dire, you can take a fuller, more measured approach to introducing agile practices. We've got some ideas for you depending on whether you're a manager or a team lead or whether you're just an interested programmer trying to lead from within the organization.

9.3 Introducing Agility: The Manager's Guide

If you're a manager or team lead, you need to start by getting the team all on board. Make it clear that *agile development is supposed to make things easier for the developers.* This is primarily for their benefit (and ultimately, the users and the organization as well). If it isn't easier, then something is wrong.

Go slowly. Remember that every little motion a leader makes is magnified by the time it hits the team.[1]

---

[1]For a great book about leading teams and honing your management skills, see *Behind Closed Doors* [RD05].

As you introduce these ideas to the team, be sure to lay out the ground rules for an agile project as described in Chapter 2, *Beginning Agility*, on page 11. Make sure everyone understands that this is how the project will be run—it's not just lip service.

Start with the stand-up meeting (see Practice 38, *Schedule Regular Face Time*, on page 151). That will give you an opportunity to get the team talking to each other and synchronized on major issues. Bring any isolated architects into the group and have them roll up their sleeves and participate (see Practice 39, *Architects Must Write Code*, on page 155). Start informal code reviews (Practice 44, *Review Code*, on page 168), and make plans to get the customer/users involved (Practice 10, *Let Customers Make Decisions*, on page 47).

Next you need to get the development infrastructure environment in order. That means adopting (or improving) the fundamental Starter Kit practices:

- Version control

- Unit testing

- Build automation

Version control needs to come before anything else. It's the first bit of infrastructure we set up on any project. Once that's set up, you need to arrange for consistent, scripted local builds for each developer that run any available unit tests as well. As that's coming online, you can start creating unit tests for all new code that's being developed and adding new tests for existing code as needed. Finally, add a continuous build machine in the background as a "backstop" to catch any remaining problems as soon as they occur.

If this is unfamiliar territory to you, run to the nearest bookstore (or www.PragmaticBookshelf.com), and get yourself a copy of *Ship It! A Practical Guide to Successful Software Projects* [RG05]; that will help you get the overall mechanics set up. The Starter Kit series can help with the details of version control, unit testing, and automation in specific environments.

With this infrastructure in place, now you need to settle into a rhythmic groove. Reread most of Chapter 4, *Delivering What Users Want*, on page 45, to get a feel for the project's timings and rhythms.

By now you have all the basics in place, so you just need to tune the practices and make them all work for *your* team. Review the material in Chapter 5, *Agile Feedback*, on page 79, as you're setting up, and then take another look at Chapter 6, *Agile Coding*, on page 101, and Chapter 7, *Agile Debugging*, on page 131, for agile approaches to daily issues.

And last, but by no means least, start introducing brown-bag lunches and the other practices as outlined in Chapter 3, *Feeding Agility*, on page 27. Work on the practices in Chapter 8, *Agile Collaboration*, on page 149, to make sure the team is working together well.

Every so often—perhaps at the end of each iteration or each release—hold a project retrospective. Get feedback *from the team*: what's working well, what needs tuning, and what things just aren't making it. If a practice you've tried isn't working out, review the *What It Feels Like* and *Keeping Your Balance* sections for that practice, and see whether there's some aspect that has fallen out of balance and can be corrected.

9.4 Introducing Agility: The Programmer's Guide

If you're not in charge of the team but would like to push them in this direction, you have a bit of a challenge ahead of you. You need to accomplish everything listed earlier in the previous section, but you're going to have to lead by example, not by decree.

As the old saying might now go, "You can lead a horse to water...but you can't make him use your favorite code editor." Unless, of course, *you* seem to be having a really good time with it. If the benefit is obvious, then your teammates will want to get in on the action.

For instance, unit testing is a good place to start. You can start by using it on your own code. Within a short time (weeks or less), you see that your code has improved—you've lowered the number of errors, improved the quality, and enhanced its robustness. You start to go home at five, and all your tasks are complete—you're not getting panic calls at night to fix bugs. The developer next to you wants to know what you're doing differently, and the word spreads. Instead of you fighting to convince the team, they are now eager to pick up the newfangled practice.

If you want to lead your team into new territory, it's only fair you go first. So start with the practices that *you* can do *right now*. Most of the practices in Chapter 2, *Beginning Agility*, on page 11, make a good start, followed by coding-oriented practices such as Practice 19, *Put Angels on Your Shoulders*, on page 81, and Practice 20, *Use It Before You Build It*, on page 85, and the practices in Chapter 6, *Agile Coding*, on page 101, and Chapter 7, *Agile Debugging*, on page 131. You can run a continuous build on your own machine and know about problems as soon as they happen. Your teammates may even think you're clairvoyant.

After a while, you might start some informal brown-bag sessions (Practice 6, *Invest in Your Team*, on page 32) and talk about the rhythms of an agile project (Practice 9, *Feel the Rhythm*, on page 41) and other topics of interest.

9.5 The End?

And that brings us to the end of the book. What happens next is entirely up to you. You can apply these practices yourself and see some personal benefit, or you can get your whole team on board and start developing better software faster and more easily.

Please visit us on the Web at `www.pragmaticprogrammer.com` where you'll find the authors' blogs and other writings, as well as links to related resources.

Thanks for reading,

Venkat & Andy

Appendix A

Resources

A.1 On the Web

Agile Developer
`http://www.agiledeveloper.com/download.aspx`
The Agile Developer download page, where you'll find articles and presentations by Venkat Subramaniam.

/\ndy's Blog
`http://toolshed.com/blog`
Andy Hunt's blog, covering a wide variety of topics and even a little software development.

Anthill
`http://www.urbancode.com/projects/anthill/default.jsp`
A tool that ensures a controlled build process (continuous integration) and promotes the sharing of knowledge within an organization.

The Art of Unix Programming
`http://www.faqs.org/docs/artu/ch04s02.html`
An excerpt from Eric Steven Raymond's *The Art of Unix Programming* book.

Continuous Integration
`http://www.martinfowler.com/articles/continuousIntegration.html`
An article that presents the benefits of continuous integration.

CruiseControl
`http://cruisecontrol.sourceforge.net`
A continuous integration tool mainly for Java applications. A C# port of this, named CruiseControl.NET, is available for the .NET platform at `http://sourceforge.net/projects/ccnet`.

Damage Control
http://dev.buildpatterns.com/trac/wiki/DamageControl
A continuous integration tool written in Ruby on Rails.

Draco.NET
http://draconet.sourceforge.net
A continuous integration tool for .NET, implemented as a Windows service.

Dependency Inversion Principle
http://c2.com/cgi/wiki?DependencyInversionPrinciple
A short article that introduces the Dependency Inversion principle.

Framework for Integration Testing
http://fit.c2.com
A collaboration tool that allows you to automatically compare customers' expectations to actual results.

Google Groups
http://groups.google.com
A website that gives you access to newsgroup discussions.

Information Radiator
http://c2.com/cgi-bin/wiki?InformationRadiator
Discusses Alistair Cockburn's Information Radiator.

Is Design Dead?
http://www.martinfowler.com/articles/designDead.html
Excellent article by Martin Fowler discusses the significance and role of design in agile development.

JUnit
http://www.junit.org
A site dedicated to software developers using JUnit or one of the other XUnit testing frameworks.

JUnitPerf
http://www.clarkware.com/software/JUnitPerf.html
A collection of JUnit test decorators used to measure the performance and scalability of functionality contained within existing JUnit tests.

NUnit
http://sourceforge.net/projects/nunit
A site dedicated to software developers using NUnit.

Object-Oriented Design Principles
http://c2.com/cgi/wiki?PrinciplesOfObjectOrientedDesign
A good collection of various object-oriented design principles.

Object-Relational Mapping

```
http://www.neward.net/ted/weblog/index.jsp?date=20041003\
#1096871640048
```

Ted Neward discusses frameworks; includes his quote "object-relational mapping is the Vietnam of computer science."

Open-Closed Principle

```
http://www.objectmentor.com/resources/articles/ocp.pdf
```

Describes the Open-Closed principle with example and limitations.

Open-Closed Principle: Short Introduction

```
http://c2.com/cgi/wiki?OpenClosedPrinciple
```

Discussions on the Open-Closed principle with opinions on the pros and cons.

Pragmatic Programming

```
http://www.pragmaticprogrammer.com
```

The Pragmatic Programmer's home page, where you'll find links to the Pragmatic Bookshelf titles (including this book), along with information for developers and managers.

Single Responsibility Principle

```
http://c2.com/cgi-bin/wiki?SingleResponsibilityPrinciple
```

Describes the Single Responsibility principle and provides links to related articles and discussions.

Software Project Management Practices: Failure versus Success

```
http://www.stsc.hill.af.mil/crosstalk/2004/10/0410Jones.html
```

Capers Jones analyzes the success and failure of 250 software projects.

Test Driven Development

```
http://c2.com/cgi/wiki?TestDrivenDevelopment
```

An introduction to Test Driven Development.

The End of Software Engineering and the Start of Economic-Cooperative Gaming

```
http://alistair.cockburn.us/crystal/articles/eoseatsoecg/
theendofsoftwareengineering.htm
```

Alistair Cockburn questions whether software development should be considered as software engineering and introduces a new model.

Tragedy on the Somme: A Second Balaclava

```
http://www.worldwar1.com/sfsomme.htm
```

This site discusses the aftermath of the Battle of Somme in Word War I.

Why Your Code Sucks

```
http://www.artima.com/weblogs/viewpost.jsp?thread=71730
```

A blog entry by Dave Astels that talks about code quality.

XProgramming.com
http://www.xprogramming.com/software.htm
A collection of resources, including testing tools.

You Aren't Gonna Need It
http://c2.com/cgi/wiki?YouArentGonnaNeedIt
Discussions on the You Aren't Gonna Need It principle with opinions on the pros and cons.

A.2 Bibliography

[Bec00]   Kent Beck. *Extreme Programming Explained: Embrace Change.* Addison-Wesley, Reading, MA, 2000.

[Cla04]   Mike Clark. *Pragmatic Project Automation: How to Build, Deploy, and Monitor Java Applications.* The Pragmatic Programmers, LLC, Raleigh, NC, and Dallas, TX, 2004.

[FBB+99]   Martin Fowler, Kent Beck, John Brant, William Opdyke, and Don Roberts. *Refactoring: Improving the Design of Existing Code.* Addison Wesley Longman, Reading, MA, 1999.

[Fow05]   Chad Fowler. *My Job Went to India: 52 Ways to Save Your Job.* The Pragmatic Programmers, LLC, Raleigh, NC, and Dallas, TX, 2005.

[GHJV95] Erich Gamma, Richard Helm, Ralph Johnson, and John Vlissides. *Design Patterns: Elements of Reusable Object-Oriented Software.* Addison-Wesley, Reading, MA, 1995.

[HT00]   Andrew Hunt and David Thomas. *The Pragmatic Programmer: From Journeyman to Master.* Addison-Wesley, Reading, MA, 2000.

[HT03]   Andrew Hunt and David Thomas. *Pragmatic Unit Testing in Java with JUnit.* The Pragmatic Programmers, LLC, Raleigh, NC, and Dallas, TX, 2003.

[HT04]   Andrew Hunt and David Thomas. *Pragmatic Unit Testing in C# with NUnit.* The Pragmatic Programmers, LLC, Raleigh, NC, and Dallas, TX, 2004.

[Jon98]   Capers Jones. *Estimating Software Costs.* McGraw Hill, 1998.

[Knu92]   Donald Ervin Knuth. *Literate Programming.* Center for the Study of Language and Information, Stanford, CA, 1992.

[Lar04]   Craig Larman. *Agile and Iterative Development: A Manager's Guide.* Addison-Wesley, Reading, MA, 2004.

[LC01]   Bo Leuf and Ward Cunningham. *The Wiki Way: Collaboration and Sharing on the Internet.* Addison-Wesley, Reading, MA, 2001.

[Lis88]   Barbara Liskov. Data abstraction and hierarchy. *SIGPLAN Notices*, 23(5), May 1988.

[Mar02]   Robert C. Martin. *Agile Software Development, Principles, Patterns, and Practices.* Prentice Hall, Englewood Cliffs, NJ, 2002.

[Mas05]   Mike Mason. *Pragmatic Version Control Using Subversion.* The Pragmatic Programmers, LLC, Raleigh, NC, and Dallas, TX, 2005.

[Mey97]   Bertrand Meyer. *Object-Oriented Software Construction.* Prentice Hall, Englewood Cliffs, NJ, second edition, 1997.

[MR84]   William A. Madden and Kyle Y. Rone. Design, development, integration: space shuttle primary flight software system. *Communications of the ACM*, 27(9):914–925, 1984.

[Rai04]   J. B. Rainsberger. *JUnit Recipes: Practical Methods for Programmer Testing.* Manning Publications Co., Greenwich, CT, 2004.

[RD05]   Johanna Rothman and Esther Derby. *Behind Closed Doors: Secrets of Great Management.* The Pragmatic Programmers, LLC, Raleigh, NC, and Dallas, TX, 2005.

[RG05]   Jared Richardson and Will Gwaltney. *Ship It! A Practical Guide to Successful Software Projects.* The Pragmatic Programmers, LLC, Raleigh, NC, and Dallas, TX, 2005.

[Roy70]   Winston W. Royce. Managing the development of large software systems. *Proceedings, IEEE WECON*, pages 1–9, August 1970.

[Sch04]   Ken Schwaber. *Agile Project Management with Scrum.* Microsoft Press, Redmond, WA, 2004.

[Sen90]   Peter Senge. *The Fifth Discipline: The Art and Practice of the Learning Organization.* Currency/Doubleday, New York, NY, 1990.

[Sha97]   Alec Sharp. *Smalltalk by Example: The Developer's Guide.* McGraw-Hill, New York, NY, 1997.

[Sub05]   Venkat Subramaniam. *.NET Gotchas.* O'Reilly & Associates, Inc., Sebastopol, CA, 2005.

[TH01]   David Thomas and Andrew Hunt. *Programming Ruby: The Pragmatic Programmer's Guide.* Addison-Wesley, Reading, MA, 2001.

[TH03]   David Thomas and Andrew Hunt. *Pragmatic Version Control Using CVS.* The Pragmatic Programmers, LLC, Raleigh, NC, and Dallas, TX, 2003.

[TH05]   David Thomas and David Heinemeier Hansson. *Agile Web Development with Rails.* The Pragmatic Programmers, LLC, Raleigh, NC, and Dallas, TX, 2005.

[You99]   Edward Yourdon. *Death March: The Complete Software Developer's Guide to Surviving "Mission Impossible" Projects.* Prentice Hall, Englewood Cliffs, NJ, 1999.

Index

Competitive Edge

Now that you've gotten an introduction to the individual practices of an agile developer, you may be interested in some of our other titles. For a full list of all of our current titles, as well as announcements of new titles, please visit www.pragmaticprogrammer.com.

Ship It!

Agility for teams. The next step from the individual focus of *Practices of an Agile Developer* is the team approach that let's you *Ship It!*, on time and on budget, without excuses. You'll see how to implement the common technical infrastructure that every project needs along with well-accepted, easy-to-adopt, best-of-breed practices that really work, as well as common problems and how to solve them.

Ship It!: A Practical Guide to Successful Software Projects
Jared Richardson and Will Gwaltney
(200 pages) ISBN: 0-9745140-4-7. $29.95

My Job Went to India

World class career advice. The job market is shifting. Your current job may be outsourced, perhaps to India or eastern Europe. But you can save your job and improve your career by following these practical and timely tips. See how to: • treat your career as a business • build your own brand as a software developer • develop a structured plan for keeping your skills up to date • market yourself to your company and rest of the industry • keep your job!

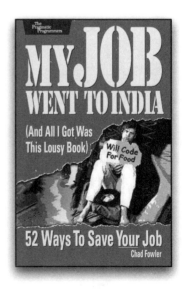

My Job Went to India: 52 Ways to Save Your Job
Chad Fowler
(208 pages) ISBN: 0-9766940-1-8. $19.95

Visit our secure online store: http://pragmaticprogrammer.com/catalog

Cutting Edge

Learn how to use the popular Ruby programming language from the Pragmatic Programmers: your definitive source for reference and tutorials on the Ruby language and exciting new application development tools based on Ruby.

The *Facets of Ruby* series includes the definitive guide to Ruby, widely known as the PickAxe book, and *Agile Web Development with Rails*, the first and best guide to the cutting-edge Ruby on Rails application framework.

Programming Ruby (The PickAxe)

The definitive guide to Ruby programming.
• Up-to-date and expanded for Ruby version 1.8. • Complete documentation of all the built-in classes, modules, methods, and standard libraries. • Learn more about Ruby's web tools, unit testing, and programming philosophy.

Programming Ruby: The Pragmatic Programmer's Guide, 2nd Edition
Dave Thomas with Chad Fowler and Andy Hunt
(864 pages) ISBN: 0-9745140-5-5. $44.95

Agile Web Development with Rails

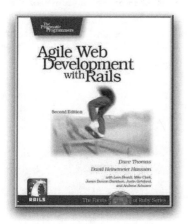

A new approach to rapid web development.
Develop sophisticated web applications quickly and easily • Learn the framework of choice for Web 2.0 developers • Use incremental and iterative development to create the web apps that users want • Get to go home on time.

**Agile Web Development with Rails
Second Edition,**
Dave Thomas and David Heinemeier Hansson
(570 pages) ISBN: 0-9776166-3-0. $39.95

Visit our secure online store: http://pragmaticprogrammer.com/catalog

The Pragmatic Bookshelf

The Pragmatic Bookshelf features books written by developers for developers. The titles continue the well-known Pragmatic Programmer style, and continue to garner awards and rave reviews. As development gets more and more difficult, the Pragmatic Programmers will be there with more titles and products to help programmers stay on top of their game.

Visit Us Online

Practices of an Agile Developer Home Page
pragmaticprogrammer.com/titles/pad
Source code from this book, errata, and other resources. Come give us feedback, too!

Register for Updates
pragmaticprogrammer.com/updates
Be notified when updates and new books become available.

Join the Community
pragmaticprogrammer.com/community
Read our weblogs, join our online discussions, participate in our mailing list, interact with our wiki, and benefit from the experience of other Pragmatic Programmers.

New and Noteworthy
pragmaticprogrammer.com/news
Check out the latest pragmatic developments in the news.

Save on the PDF

Save more than 60% on the PDF version of this book. Owning the paper version of this book entitles you to purchase the PDF version for only $7.50 (regularly $20). That's a saving of more than 60%. The PDF is great for carrying around on your laptop. It's hyperlinked, has color, and is fully searchable. Buy it now at pragmaticprogrammer.com/coupon

Contact Us

Phone Orders:	1-800-699-PROG (+1 919 847 3884)
Online Orders:	www.pragmaticprogrammer.com/catalog
Customer Service:	orders@pragmaticprogrammer.com
Non-English Versions:	translations@pragmaticprogrammer.com
Pragmatic Teaching:	academic@pragmaticprogrammer.com
Author Proposals:	proposals@pragmaticprogrammer.com